PLANTING

A CHURCH

WITHOUT

LOSING

YOUR

SOUL

Nine

Questions

for the

Spiritually

Formed

Pastor

TIM MOREY

FOREWORD BY
SCOTT W. SUNQUIST

ivp
Academic
An imprint of InterVarsity Press
Downers Grove, Illinois

InterVarsity Press
P.O. Box 1400, Downers Grove, IL 60515-1426
ivpress.com
email@ivpress.com

InterVarsity Press® is the book-publishing division of InterVarsity Christian Fellowship/USA®, a movement of students and faculty active on campus at hundreds of universities, colleges, and schools of nursing in the United States of America, and a member movement of the International Fellowship of Evangelical Students. For information about local and regional activities, visit intervarsity.org.

While any stories in this book are true, some names and identifying information may have been changed to protect the privacy of individuals.

Author photo by David Herrera

Cover design and image composite: Cindy Kiple
Interior design: Daniel van Loon
Images: bonsai tree: © Peter Dazeley / The Image Bank / Getty Images

ISBN 978-0-8308-5279-6 (print)
ISBN 978-0-8308-5343-4 (digital)

Printed in the United States of America ∞

InterVarsity Press is committed to ecological stewardship and to the conservation of natural resources in all our operations. This book was printed using sustainably sourced paper.

Library of Congress Cataloging-in-Publication Data
A catalog record for this book is available from the Library of Congress.

| P | 21 | 20 | 19 | 18 | 17 | 16 | 15 | 14 | 13 | 12 | 11 | 10 | 9 | 8 | 7 | 6 | 5 | 4 | 3 | 2 | 1 |
| Y | 37 | 36 | 35 | 34 | 33 | 32 | 31 | 30 | 29 | 28 | 27 | 26 | 25 | 24 | 23 | 22 | 21 | 20 |

"Tim Morey did a courageous thing. He told the truth. In a space that is often filled with the retelling of airbrushed success stories, Tim wrote a book that revealed the difficulties often found in church planting and the effects those difficulties can have on church planters and their families. But Tim doesn't leave us there. His book enumerates many practicalities that will guide a church planter to avoid the worst and thrive in the work of church planting. *Planting a Church Without Losing Your Soul* is a refreshing book and a significant contribution to the church planting conversation."

Ed Stetzer, professor and dean at Wheaton College, executive director of the Wheaton College Billy Graham Center

"There are very few books on the subject of church planting that I would say are a must-read for church planters—but this is one of them. Tim Morey writes transparently as he surfaces the war wounds common to the assignment and helps the reader understand the deeper issues that surround and exacerbate the pain. As I read Tim's thoughtful guidance, I found myself continually saying, 'Yes, yes!' as I saw my own story recounted in his words. Buy this book. Read this book. And give this book to every church planter that you know."

Jeff Christopherson, cofounder and missiologist at the Send Institute, executive director of Church Planting Canada

"Tim Morey's work takes a much-needed turn off the church planting highway of assessments, structured pathways, and preconceived definitions of success. Rather, Morey takes on the honest, painful, and difficult task of helping us unpack our own emotional and spiritual well-being. The probing questions and practical responses transcend the particularities of social location and expose the heart and spirit of those who seek to partner with Christ in planting a community of faith."

Dwight Radcliff, Pannell Center for African American Church Studies, assistant professor of theology, mission, and culture, Fuller Theological Seminary

"After decades of planting churches and training planters, I've come to believe that the first work of planters is to ground our identity in God, lest we become possessed by our image. I can say one thing unequivocally about this book: Tim, with hard-won wisdom, identifies ten areas that are paramount for leaders to contemplate and engage, if we want to have a life worth imitating and not fall captive to the powers. This book is for planters who are in it for the long haul."

JR Woodward, national director of the V3 Movement, author of *Creating a Missional Culture*

"Tim Morey has cracked the code for *Planting a Church Without Losing Your Soul*. It is the genius of Jesus: the responses to life and leadership flow from the heart. I have been involved in church planting for forty years and can tell you that Tim has crucial things to say. I hope this book enables the next generation of church planters to be simultaneously fruitful and well with their soul."

Todd D. Hunter, bishop of the Anglican diocese Churches for the Sake of Others, author of *Our Character at Work*

"Tim Morey peels back the curtain to provide a glimpse into the hearts and minds of church planters. Tackling foundational emotional and spiritual essentials, this work is an encouragement to potential and on-the-job new church developers alike. You will see yourself in Tim's stories and be guided through reflection to guard against burnout (or worse) and helped to cultivate your inner life as you plant. I recommend *Planting a Church Without Losing Your Soul* for healthy personal development while starting and growing churches."

Robert E. Logan, author of *The Church Planting Journey* and *The Discipleship Difference*

TO CHUCK PRICE,

who not only mentored me into ministry
but taught me to pastor in healthy, sustainable ways

CONTENTS

FOREWORD

Scott W. Sunquist

PROBABLY THE MOST IMPORTANT ISSUE facing the church in the West is how to plant churches that are healthy Christian communities themselves and are vital to their local communities. Even with all of the great revivals of evangelicalism in the last half of the twentieth century, those under thirty years of age are only about 8 percent evangelical today.[1] The past few decades have seen an explosion of interest in church planting, whole church planting movements, and professional training for church planters. Yet the decline continues. Something more is needed.

The reality is that healthy leaders plant healthy churches. Evangelistic leaders plant churches that seek to evangelize. Leaders who care about justice and the marginalized—well, you know the rest.

And so Tim Morey has taken on one of the central concerns for Christians in North America. The critical place of *leaders* in the health and growth of Christianity is the subtle background theme that is woven throughout this volume. Leadership is absolutely critical, but it is not just a matter of what a leader does. Of greatest importance is who a leader *is* and what a leader *is becoming*. Tim leads us into this world of a leader becoming, and that includes becoming comfortable with herself or himself.

When I was in the planning stages of starting a church planting program, I did a year of informal research to find out what the main subjects were that needed to be covered by a theological seminary. What should we offer to help build strong and competent church planters? I learned a lot. However, what caught me by surprise was the universal need for spiritual formation—deep personal work in the life of the church planter—to prevent depression, failure, and even suicide.

It was then that I realized planting a church is very difficult. The stress on personal lives and on families and friendships is great. Many people lose their best friends who decide not to be part of this "new adventure." Marriages are stressed when people stop coming to "your" church. And then there is the problem of money. One denominational executive mentioned flatly: "We had two church planters commit suicide last year."

This volume deals with vital issues for the church in North America—vital issues that focus on the foundation for healthy churches, which is the formation of the leader. Biblical, pastoral, narrative, historical, and even psychological in orientation, Tim moves easily from one mode to the next. His variegated approach is necessary for a volume like this. Some of us will connect directly with the stories of failure or the surprising stories of success. Some of us will be moved and changed as we see passages of Scripture in a new light, brought to bear on the life of the church planter.

There is another genius to this book. Tim's humility in talking about his own failures makes it easy for us, the readers, to empathize and to learn from his mistakes (and some successes). This book will help us grow in empathy, one of the lost virtues in our contemporary world of multitasking and thoughtless quick responses on social media. And, by the way, Tim talks about *empathy and suffering* in chapter three. It may be a good idea to start in that chapter.

As I was reading through this book I wanted to pick up the phone and thank Tim for writing a book on spirituality for seminary presidents! No, this is not written for folks like myself, but I found myself grateful for what is written for a different audience. So many of the important lessons of life, especially the life of a leader—sacred rhythms, suffering, humility, power, pace, obscurity—are found in these pages.

Please read this book slowly and talk to your spouse, spiritual director, family, or church small group about it. Mull over the concepts. Pick up your Bible and look at the passages for yourself. And pray.

I should also add that this book is part of a quartet of books about church planting. The first book, *Why Church?*, gave an overview of what the church (or a local church) can and should be.[2] The second, *Sent to Flourish*, is a compilation of chapters written by a diverse group of church planters.[3] This third volume, *Planting a Church Without Losing Your Soul*, is the critical one, for if the church planter is not healthy, all the right theology and strategy is for naught. The fourth volume will be on the missional pastor—another long-overdue book.

Lesslie Newbigin, missionary to India and to England, said on a number of occasions that the local church must be a signpost of the kingdom. However, this will happen only if the churches are led by leaders who are being made more into the likeness of Jesus Christ. Tim Morey is a helpful guide for us on that journey.

SCOTT W. SUNQUIST
president, Gordon-Conwell Theological Seminary

WHAT DOES A SPIRITUALLY FORMED CHURCH PLANTER LOOK LIKE?

I WAS A TWENTY-FIVE-YEAR-OLD, newly married seminarian when I began to sense I was called to plant a church.

I shared my growing sense of call with the professor of the church planting elective I was taking (he also served on our denomination's church planting team), and before I knew it Samantha and I were stuffing warm clothes into a suitcase and boarding an airplane for a church planter assessment center in Connecticut. As state after frozen state passed beneath us, I looked out the window and dreamed of the church we might plant in our hometown of San Diego. In my mind, the church was full of excited young adults with an unquenchable passion for God's kingdom. I couldn't wait to see it become a reality.

At the assessment center our days were spent in the basement fellowship hall of an old Baptist church. Church planter candidates gave sermons, shared their calls to ministry, underwent numerous uncomfortably personal interviews, participated in group projects and case studies (so assessors could watch both our reasoning skills and our ability to work with others), and were evaluated by the resident psychologist.

At night Samantha and I would return, exhausted, to the home of an elderly widow who had offered to put us up in her guest room. No matter how late we got in, she would greet us with hot tea and warm conversation. I would smile and listen, but mostly I was thinking about my fellow assessees. They were so gifted in so many ways, and I was intimidated. *How did I get here?* I wondered. *I don't measure up.*

We endured three days of being under the microscope, and then on the morning of day four, they gave us the verdict. In the view of the assessors—a group of seasoned planters and pastors—did we have the competencies needed to plant a church?

When it was our turn to hear the verdict, they steered us to the director's office instead of into the room where the other assessees were meeting. *That makes sense,* I thought. *They send the ones they are rejecting to the director so he can tell them in person.*

The director smiled warmly and shook our hands. "Have a seat," he said, as he took his place on the other side of the desk. Samantha and I sat silent and stiff, holding hands, eyes forward. I could barely breathe.

"Let me get right to it," the director said. "We believe God is calling you to plant that church in San Diego. And we're ready to get behind you—with money." I just stared. I was expecting to hear, "You're too young, but a few more years of experience and maybe, just maybe, you'll be ready." I could tell without looking that Samantha's eyes, like mine, were filling with tears, and I slowly became aware that we were squeezing each other's hands a little too tightly. We were on the brink of a great adventure.

A lot has happened in the years since then. We did plant, eventually. But God in his mercy saw fit to restrain me, closing the door to that first church plant in San Diego (my first of many heartbreaking moments as a planter). Instead, he placed me in a large Los Angeles church as a staff pastor for the next five years.

Before long I made peace with what I thought of as a ministry detour. *I'm young and still pretty inexperienced,* I thought. *I need to develop sharper ministry skills.* While that was true, I came to learn it wasn't primarily ministry skills that I needed to develop.

FROM DREAM TO DETOUR TO REALITY

The bigger need was my spiritual readiness. By this I don't mean to imply that I was drifting deeply into sin or didn't have a solid walk with God—it wasn't that. Rather, there were areas where I didn't know it yet, but God needed to further develop my *spiritual competencies* if I was going to survive the church-planting gauntlet.

My insecurities topped the list. The ways they manifested are painful to think about: my need to be noticed and praised; my shortness of patience with those I shepherded; my need to appear "successful" (whatever that means); my tendency to overmanage our lay leaders lest they make a mistake, and under-praise them lest credit for successes get diverted away from me. There was, and is, so much that God needed to work out in me.

There were, indeed, a host of church-planter characteristics that God needed to develop in me before I planted, but they weren't the ones I thought. What God primarily needed to develop in me were not stronger ministry skills but stronger spiritual competencies.

Difficult though it was at the time, without the lessons those years provided, I hate to think of the mess I would have made of that first church, and the harm I would have brought on myself and those around me.

WHAT *DOES* IT TAKE TO BE A CHURCH PLANTER?

Every church planter assessment looks for certain vocational competencies that are vital to planting a healthy church. *Can this person gather people? Can they organize those people once they are gathered? Lead them into a God-shaped vision of the future? Preach and teach the Bible in a way that brings life change?* Through questionnaires, interviews, references, case studies, and a host of diagnostics, an assessment center can gather enough evidence of past behavior to get a reasonable idea of what a planter's future behavior is going to look like.[1]

In addition to these vocational competencies, assessments evaluate a whole realm of capabilities we might call spiritual competencies. These are every bit as vital, if not more so, than the vocational competencies. They are also more difficult to measure, as they probe areas of our spiritual readiness that can lie deep beneath the surface. They have to do not just with our behaviors but with the underlying motivations, agendas, and scripts that drive those behaviors.

- Am I being formed in such a way that I am capable of carrying out this work, and carrying it out well?
- Am I ready to minister for the marathon, and not just the sprint?
- Will I be experienced as a blessing and not a curse by those I lead? By my family? By myself?
- Can I minister from a place of deep joy, even in times of real difficulty?

Those are the big questions this book seeks to answer. *What are the spiritual competencies that I as a church planter need to develop, and how might I begin to seek out and lean into Jesus' transforming work in me in these vital areas?*

In the pages that follow, I want to propose a number of specific areas where we as church planters might ask Jesus to form us. While these growth areas would no doubt be of benefit to any pastor, many will find that the challenges and temptations of ministry are more pronounced in the unique environment of a freshly planted church. Many of the subtle, built-in safeguards of a more established church— a history of how things have and haven't been done, an existing board of elders, congregational expectations for how pastors conduct themselves—simply don't exist. The church-planting pastor inherently wields an uncomfortable amount of power.

What's more, these spiritual capabilities are areas where we will be unable to simply muscle our way through, or at least unable to muscle through for very long. No, they lie too deep in our souls for that.

These are areas we develop only through actively pursuing our *own* spiritual formation, leaning into these given areas, and asking Jesus in his grace to grow us.

Finally, we should note that these competencies are not simply traits that we either have or do not have but rather areas that we can *develop*. In fact, we may find that Jesus' work of shaping these capabilities in us may be the most important work he does in our church.

THE YEARS SINCE, AND WHO I AM

In 2003, when we planted Life Covenant Church in Torrance, California, we were still young and pretty green, but we had a little better handle on what both church health and our own spiritual health looked like. It was, and continues to be, messy. But it's a much healthier mess than it would have been otherwise.

Leading Life Cov (as we sometimes call it) has been both more joyous and more difficult than I imagined it would be. In the rest of the book I'll be talking mostly about the difficulties, so it's probably good to mention at the outset that the experience has been brimming with joy as well, and also give a bit of a picture of who I am and the ministry context from which I write.

Life Cov is a church that is passionate about grace, about being a community on mission, and about being disciples whom Jesus is transforming into his likeness. We have grown as disciples and made disciples. We've baptized new believers in the Pacific, in hot tubs, and in backyard swimming pools. We've helped homeless families get into homes, helped children come up in the nurture of the Lord, served our local schools, and provided meals for local kids whose families are so dependent on school lunches that they don't eat on the weekends. It's been fruitful in dozens of beautiful yet modest ways.

And though we aren't a large congregation (about two hundred), we have been blessed to be a very active parenting church as well. At the time of this writing we have given birth to five daughter or granddaughter churches in Southern California, and close to two hundred in Mozambique, Africa.

Along the way God has seen fit to put me in close proximity with many other church planters as well. For a number of years I served on the national church planting team for our denomination (the Evangelical Covenant Church), primarily as the director of our assessment center, but also as a trainer and coach for new planters. I've taught and coached church planters for other denominations, too, and for the past six years I've served Fuller Theological Seminary as an adjunct professor and steering committee member for the school's church planting initiative.

These experiences have also been a joy, and they have deepened my love for new churches and for those who lead them. This book, in fact, came out of the observation of a colleague about my love for church planters. "Whatever the topic," he said, "you always seem to bring it back to the health of the church planter. Maybe that should be your next book."

To that end, at the close of each chapter you will find a few questions designed to move the planter toward deeper reflection and concrete application. Or better yet, these questions can be utilized to help a planter process this material with their coach, or to help a group of planters providing each other with peer support to process the material together.

And while church planters are the primary audience for this book, I trust that more established pastors and ministry leaders, as well as denominational and network leaders who work with pastors, will find these same competencies helpful in their vocations. While the details may take a little different shape in a church plant, I believe what's written here is applicable across any number of ministries.

Finally, I hope it goes without saying that I don't write this as one who has figured it all out. As will become clear in the pages to follow, I offer these insights with profound humility as one who is better at identifying my growth areas than mastering them. What I share here are merely patterns that I have observed in my own life and in those planters with whom I've been blessed to journey.

My prayer is that God would use this book to make you a healthier, more vibrant, and more fulfilled church planter. What's more, I pray that your work might be a joy—to you, your family, and those you lead. And I pray that the fruit of your work might echo into eternity.

1

HOW TO BE BOTH A PASTOR AND A PERSON

Pastors don't get in trouble because they forget they are pastors.
They get in trouble because they forget they are people.

ARCHIBALD HART

That is why, for Christ's sake, I delight in weaknesses.

PAUL THE APOSTLE (2 CORINTHIANS 12:10)

"YOU ARE DOING THIS ALL WRONG," Charlie said gently.

My spiritual director (or as I liked to think of him, my personal monk) sat there quietly, a kind smile on his face. His hands rested lightly on crossed legs. A flickering candle sat on the coffee table between us, and Charlie's pronouncement seemed to hover in the air above the flame.

"You have become a *warehouse*, storing and holding all the church's problems. But God never intended that. He intends you to be a *warehouseman.*"

Another couple had left our young church plant—one of the few families that had children. They loved the church but were concerned that our fledgling children's ministry would not be able to adequately minister to their kids as they grew. I couldn't argue—we were so new at this, and the church had just a handful of kids. Our plan was solid, and I was confident that as more families with children came to the church that it would be just a few years before we would have a robust ministry for kids. But how could I really know, and how could parents really know? *And how will we ever get there if families with children won't stick?* I was discouraged and worried, and didn't know how we could escape the vicious cycle we found ourselves in.

Charlie sat patiently, a smile barely perceptible on his lips, content to let his words gain weight as we sat in the silence.

"What do you mean?" I finally asked.

"You are holding onto all of the church's problems, Tim—storing them in your mind and heart as if your soul is a giant warehouse. But you aren't *capable* of holding all these concerns. Nor are you meant to be. God alone can hold the church's problems."

Charlie paused again, his easy demeanor matching the counsel he was giving. "You are not to be the warehouse that holds all the problems but a *warehouseman*. Your job is to get on your forklift, pick up the church's problems, set them down in the warehouse, and then drive away. As long as you try to do what only God can do, you're going to be anxious and exhausted."

Charlie paused, and then leaned forward for emphasis. *"You need to let yourself be the pastor, and let God be God."*

LEARNING HOW TO NOT BE GOD

Zack Eswine, in his important book *The Imperfect Pastor*, writes, "I became a pastor. But I didn't know how to be one. The Serpent saw this. He seized his opportunity. 'You can be like God,' he said. And I, the fool, believed him."[1]

Part of me reads that line and resonates with it, while another part protests, "No. I don't do that, do I?" Eswine goes on to detail the ways that we try to be everywhere for everyone (omnipresence), fix everything for everyone (omnipotence), and have all the answers for everyone (omniscience), and I realize just how much of my vocation as a church planter is my trying to do what I cannot possibly do.

Dr. Chris Adams is director of the Center for Vocational Ministry at Azusa Pacific University and a researcher for two of the largest studies on pastoral health to date. For one of these studies they contracted a consultant whose job it is to determine what competencies are needed for various marketplace jobs, and they asked him to evaluate the role of pastor. Recognizing that pastors wear of a lot of hats, he expected the list to be long, yet he came back shocked at his own findings: a staggering list of *sixty-five* core competencies a person needs to lead a church. "No one can be good at all of these things," he said. "This is a setup to feel inadequate. *Who would ever want to do this job?*"

Adams reports that all this contributes to the danger of chronically elevated stress among pastors, which creates substantial wear and tear on a pastor's mind and body over time. Pastors have higher rates of anxiety and depression than the general population. They have poorer lifestyle-related health markers, including higher rates of obesity, hypertension, diabetes, and metabolic syndrome. Research would indicate that at any given time, one-third of pastors are experiencing burnout and/or depression. Only one-fourth of pastors, Adams' research finds, finish well with vitality.[2]

Given the additional stressors for pastors engaged in the work of establishing a new church, there is good reason for church planters to pay particular attention to their need to intentionally learn to minister in ways that are healthy and life-giving. In addition to the typical list of pastoral duties, consider the complexities in a church plant:

- Planters have the start-up responsibilities of an entrepreneur as well as regular pastoral duties.
- The planter is most often a solo pastor, not part of a staff.

- Church systems are not yet established, which means greater effort in nearly everything.
- Many church planters have less accountability than established pastors—either to an elder board within the church or, for many, to denominational leaders.
- Church planters have few (or zero) established leaders to share the work.
- Planters face the constant pressure of wondering whether the church will make it.
- Planters are not always appreciated by local colleagues, who often feel threatened by the presence of a new church.

THE ELIJAH SYNDROME

Recognizing our need is our first challenge. For most, the next challenge is to learn to receive care from God and those agents he would use in bringing us care. I find a good model for the kind of holistic care we need to receive from God in Elijah in 1 Kings 19.[3]

The real power in this chapter comes out when you contrast it with the chapter it follows. In 1 Kings 18, Elijah has just finished one of the most spectacular ministry moments in all of Scripture—his miraculous victory over the prophets of Baal. Against overwhelming odds, a defiant Elijah taunts his opponents in an epic showdown to see whose God or gods are the strongest. Fire literally comes down from heaven, and Yahweh's victory is decisive, leaving no doubt as to who the real God is and what his power can accomplish.

Yet as chapter 19 opens, instead of finding Elijah elated and triumphant, we find him exhausted, discouraged, and fearing for his life. *How can this be?* the reader wonders. How can one experience such a display of God's power in one moment, then turn around and doubt his power in the next?

Our church members might scratch their heads, but pastors have no problem relating to this story. Pastors routinely find themselves physically and emotionally spent come Monday morning, a phenomenon I've actually heard referred to as Elijah Syndrome. The adrenaline dump that follows a significant ministry event can leave one's mind and body feeling heavy and sluggish. Thoughts of discouragement and inadequacy seem to carry more weight. Anticipation of the coming work week can feel daunting.

Intuitively, I would think that only the failures would drain us, while successful ministry ventures would be nothing but life-giving. Yet experience teaches us something different. Even good ministry can leave us depleted. I'm learning to anticipate that after the adrenaline dump that follows a significant ministry event, I may find myself markedly tired—physically, emotionally, and spiritually. On those days, I should be especially cautious in trusting my already fickle emotions.

That's where we find Elijah. Feeling depleted and defeated, he does physically what many of us do emotionally: "He runs for his life" (1 Kings 19:3). Elijah runs, traveling a full day's journey into the wilderness. There, echoing the sentiments of many ministers to follow, he yells at the heavens, "I have had enough! Take my life, I am no better than my ancestors" (v. 4). Then he lies down in the shade of a bush and falls asleep.

Do you hear any of yourself in Elijah's cry? I've expressed to God, in slightly different words, each of his sentiments at one time or another:

Fatigue: "I'm exhausted, burned out! I can't go on doing this."

Discouragement, tipping into despair: "This job is sucking away my life! I'd be too ashamed to quit, and I don't know what else I would do. But I need out. Please God, let me do something else."

Self-doubt: "I'm not any good at this—no better than those who have tried and failed before me. I certainly don't compare to [insert name of superpastor *du jour*]. Am I really accomplishing anything? I should quit ministry and become a banker."

Into this struggle, God provides care for Elijah in four distinct ways—areas of care that we need as well.

Physical. "Get up and eat," the angel says to Elijah. Elijah wakes to the smell of freshly baked bread next to a jar of water. And then we read what, for any who are acquainted with deep, heart-level fatigue and its accompanying discouragement, are some of the most beautiful words in Scripture: "He ate the meal and went back to sleep" (v. 6, MSG).

Sometimes, the most spiritual thing you and I can do is take a nap.

Sometimes, the most spiritual thing you and I can do is take a nap.

Before his death I had the opportunity to take a class with Dr. Dallas Willard. As a class, we stayed together for two weeks in a monastery, studying and practicing the spiritual disciplines. It was a life-changing experience.

"Your first assignment while we are here," Dallas said on day one, "is to get ten hours of sleep each night." Ten hours? We all looked around at each other, dumbfounded. This was a doctoral program, which required a ton of work, and also required that students be in full-time ministry. When could we even remember getting that much sleep? It sounded crazy. "If you can't actually sleep," he continued, "at least be in bed for ten hours, and spend the awake time reading and praying."

The next morning at breakfast everyone groused about how difficult it was trying to sleep that much, how early you had to go to bed even to attempt it, and so on. The second morning we still groused, but most of us reported a slightly better experience. By day three, people were talking about feeling more rested than they were used to. By the end of the week we couldn't imagine going back to living on as little sleep as we had before.

The physical is spiritual. Do you notice that when Elijah is at his point of exhaustion, God doesn't even bother speaking to him?

Before he does anything else, God just attends to Elijah's basic, bodily needs: food, water, and sleep. I don't think it is too far of a reach to say that prior to this, Elijah is not even at a place where he can hear what God has to say to him.

It's a truth so simple that we easily forget it: *you and I have a body.* Everything we will ever do in God's service will take place in the body he has given us. Therefore, it is vitally important that we treat ourselves as human persons—bodily beings who simply cannot get on without proper rhythms of rest, work, hydration, and nutrition.

As noted above, the average pastor has poorer health markers than the general population, including higher rates of obesity, heart disease, and metabolic syndrome. While for some, heredity is a contributing factor, we have to note that for many of us, these are directly related to lifestyle choices.

Yes, our work is high in stress, which causes our bodies to hold onto more fat than we would like, and the random nature of our schedules makes it harder to plan for exercise and healthy eating. Yet overeating and unhealthy eating are the norm for many in ministry. Perhaps it's because some part of us thinks we are invincible—that God will let us slide on our poor physical habits because the work we are doing is important. Or maybe it's because in America, gluttony has become an acceptable vice. Think about it: if our congregation found out we were coping with ministry stress by drinking too much, there would be great concern, and if we didn't turn it around quickly, we might even lose our ministry. But whose church is going to call them out for chronic overeating? It has become too easy for us to get away with being poor stewards of our bodies.

This is why attending to diet, exercise, and sleep should be thought of as spiritual disciplines, not just physical ones. In fact, in recent years when I have spoken on self-care, attending to our bodily health has become one of the top five disciplines I prescribe for every church planter.[4]

So let me ask you, friend, have you considered that part of the care Jesus invites you to is simply to care for your body? To eat well, to exercise, to sleep?

The angel's words reinforce this: "Get up and eat, *for the journey is too much for you*" (1 Kings 19:7). You are human, Elijah, and you have a body. Acknowledge it, care for it, and respect its limits.

Emotional. The second thing that strikes me in this story is how tenderly God deals with Elijah.

Twice God invites Elijah to speak, and twice he listens while Elijah rants: "I have been very zealous for the Lord God Almighty. The Israelites have rejected your covenant, torn down your altars, and put your prophets to death with the sword. I am the only one left, and now they are trying to kill me too" (v. 10, 14).

God creates space for Elijah to vent his honest emotions, and then he listens.

If I were God, my response would likely have been full of correction. "Do you think you might be overstating things, Eli? Perhaps your perspective is a little distorted. Let's go statement by statement through what you said and evaluate its accuracy."

But there is no rebuke for Elijah's outburst, no expression of divine disappointment for how quickly Elijah moves from ministry euphoria to evaporating faith, no correction of Elijah's wrong-headed reasoning. Like a loving parent, God simply invites Elijah to tell him what is wrong. God hears Elijah's anger, fear, and sorrow, and he holds it.

Many of us, when shaking our fist at God, are only made angrier by the gentleness of his presence. We want God to react—either to apologize for allowing ministry to beat us up, or to rebuke us for our insolence. But I've come to feel in my spirit that in those moments God is giving me what I truly need but am not sober enough to see: space to be angry, to be hurt, to be afraid, to be sad. And like a loving father, God simply holds my big emotions while I rant.

Isn't this what the Psalms teach us, that God can handle—strike that—that he *actually wants to handle*—our raw emotion? *"How long Lord, how long?"* Nearly half the Psalms are songs of pain or anger—many of them blaming God. If the Psalms are there to teach us to pray, then certainly we must conclude that God is ready to meet and minister to us in the midst of our strong emotions, not just after we have gotten them under control.

> God is ready to meet and minister to us in the midst of our strong emotions.

C. S. Lewis, in his own journey back from deep grief, described God's gentle presence as a special sort of silence—not the silence of a God who is absent or who has bolted the door in response to our knocking, but a silence that patiently and lovingly listens to our pain. "It is more," Lewis says, "like a silent, not uncompassionate gaze," which seems to say, "Peace, child; you don't understand."[5]

I struggle here. I come from a family and a church tradition that values being composed, together, and self-controlled, and I want others to see me as a leader who has it together. I prefer to master my emotions first and talk about them only after they have been safely contained.

But the truth is, God can handle my meltdowns. As pastors we need to take a page from the Psalms and learn to come to him with raw, unfiltered emotion. Perhaps more important, we need to come to a place where we know in our bones that our Father actually *wants* that, and that he is happy to sit with us in our overwhelmed state.

And furthermore, many of us need to admit that we are underdeveloped in this area, to the point that if we are going to grow, we are going to need to enlist someone's help. That is why we insist that our planters are either in therapy or spiritual direction all the time. Don't wait until you break—intentionally develop the spiritual muscle to let God care for your emotional needs.

Spiritual. When Elijah is ready to receive it, God speaks: "Go out and stand on the mountain in the presence of the Lord, for the Lord is about to pass by" (v. 11).

The mountain in question is Mount Horeb. There, centuries earlier, a barefoot shepherd standing before a burning bush received his call to ministry. Years later that same shepherd-turned-deliverer stood on the mountain and received the Ten Commandments amid a full-blown light show. That time the whole mountain shook as it blazed with fire, black clouds, and deep darkness. From the fire the Lord's voice bellowed, displaying with terrifying effectiveness the power of God to accomplish his purposes (Deut 4:10-14; Ex 19:16-19). Did this history, coupled with Elijah's recent experience of God's power, shape his expectations of how God would meet him, of the shape his calling would take?

What, I wonder, has shaped my expectations of how God would meet me, of how he would shape my call? My faith was nurtured in megachurches where success was made visible by a full parking lot, multiple services, and impeccable production quality. Naturally, I expected that as I grew in ministry, God would meet me in similar ways and call me to similar tasks.

As I grew disillusioned with that world (unfairly so, in many ways), I became enamored of the emerging wave of church planters reaching new generations in fresh ways. In that world, success was made visible less by size than by innovation, multiplication, and an ethos that valued rawness and authenticity over production quality. This world, too, subtly shaped my expectations of how God would meet me, and how my calling would develop.

Famously, God does not meet Elijah in the way he expects. Like Moses before him, God has Elijah wait in a cleft in the rock for God to pass by. Like Moses, Elijah sees God move in wind, a shaking earth, and fire. But unlike the case of Moses, God doesn't speak. His voice only comes after the displays of strength have ended, in a gentle whisper.

It is as if God is saying, "You want me to come to you in a familiar display of power so you can be assured I am bigger than the powers you are now running from. I've done that already, Elijah, and you didn't recognize it. But I am doing something different with you. You are not Moses, and his story is not your story. You are Elijah, and you have to trust me to write your story too."

How many of us enter church planting looking for God to give us the same story he gave someone else, a story we admire and want to see written over our lives as well? The story we want might be that of the leader of a younger, fresher kind of megachurch, or leader of a network of house churches that excels in disciple-making, or of a missional congregation doing rich incarnational ministry among urban hipsters, or of an inner-city powerhouse prophetically breaking down ethnic and cultural barriers as they unmask systemic injustice. All these stories are great, and each one is needed in the kingdom. But the story you are looking to write may or may not be the story God has for you.

When God is ready to speak, are you willing to hear what he has to say? Are you ready to have him minister to you spiritually, even if it entails him saying things or leading you in ways that differ from the story you are wanting?

When we started Life Cov, our intention was to reach unchurched people. And yes, we have reached some, but more than any other group, we have found that our church is deeply attractive to those we have come to call the dechurched: people who may or may not already have a saving relationship with God, but have been wounded or burnt out on religion and long since walked away from the church—and often from God too.

Even though I loved these people deeply, for the first two years of our church's life it frustrated me that God was bringing them instead of the more truly unchurched. "We want to see more people who have absolutely no church background!" I would tell God. "Why do we keep getting all these wounded Christians and ex-Christians? We want to reach hardcore pagans!"

One day while ranting in prayer, I sensed the need to be quiet and listen. In the quiet I clearly sensed the Spirit saying in my spirit, "Tim, these people aren't coming to you by accident. You have these people because I am sending them, and this is going to be a significant part of the ministry I have for you. Embrace it, rejoice in it, and pastor your people."

As I reflected on this, it began to make sense. My background was such that I understood the dechurched well, and they seemed to sense that. And as a result of their presence, our church was growing in grace and able to receive them well. Rather than greeting them with judgment, we were able to honor their stories, value their gifts, and give them a place to belong and to serve and to heal.

God does not always meet us in the way we are expecting or wanting, but he always meets us in the way that we need.

Relational. "I am all alone," Elijah says, and no doubt he believes this to be true. But God meets him in this, too, giving him two kings as allies and a committed disciple to be his partner and successor. He also alerts Elijah to the presence of *seven thousand* others he was not aware of who are committed to the Lord as well (v. 15-18).

I find it striking that God does not feel it is sufficient to assure Elijah of his presence, as I might expect that the gentle whisper would be the final word in this story. But God goes a step further and assures Elijah of the presence of other allies as well. Centuries later, Jesus would give similar words of assurance to an anxious Paul, as he works to plant a church in the difficult city of Corinth. "Do not be afraid; keep on speaking, do not be silent. For I am with you, and no one is going to attack and harm you, *because I have many people in this city*" (Acts 18:9-10).

Jesus promises that he will be with us as we go about his work, and we can be confident he will. But we need to remember that one of the ways he cares for us is by providing us with other people too.

"The number one hazard for pastors is isolation," according to Dr. Chris Adams.[6] Pastoral leadership, we learn fairly quickly, is isolating. We carry secrets we cannot share, make decisions that will make us unpopular with those whose affirmation we desire, and endure jabs and bruises that we have to keep hidden lest we throw congregants under the bus.

Church planters, as a subset of pastors, are almost by definition isolated. Most serve on their own, not as part of a larger staff team. Even those who are blessed with a solid core of lay leaders (and this is far from guaranteed) may feel limited in what we can share with them about other church members, or about our own fears and frustrations with the church, lest we undermine their confidence in our ministry too. Other area pastors may or may not extend a hand of friendship, as many see a new church plant as a threat to their own fragile ego or ministry. It is easy as a planter to feel alone.

> *One of the ways Jesus cares for us is by providing us with other people.*

This has huge implications for us as church planters. It means that you and I must actively combat isolation. One way we do that is to make the practice of community a non-optional spiritual discipline in our lives.

Can we cultivate community with those in our church? Yes. By all means, cultivate relationships that are deep and meaningful with people in your church who you find safe and life-giving. I can't imagine that I would still be a church planter if I didn't have some great friends in our congregation. But it's important to cultivate outside relationships, too, as relationships in the church will inherently have limits that stop short of what you need.

As much as I trust my friends in the church, there are certain pains, certain fears, certain discouragements that I cannot share in full, lest it color the way they see a fellow congregant. Even with my wife, who is my favorite person to process my pains with, I'm learning to be wise in what I do and don't share so I don't unfairly burden her or alter how she views someone she will see every Sunday. Consequently, I find that the longer I'm in ministry, the more I value the life-giving relationships I have with my pastor friends.

To this end, one remedy our denomination wisely employs is to organize its church planters into regional clusters. Every other month, we sit together over a two-hour brown bag lunch to tell stories of laughter and of heartache, to learn from each other, and to pray. Similarly, I convene a monthly coffee for our city's pastors, which has become an important time of reprieve for many of us. There is something great about going into a room where you know everyone at the table understands your life before you say a word. The people in my church don't always understand what my life is like, but my pastor buddies do.

Physical, emotional, spiritual, relational. Do you believe that God *wants* to care for you in each of these ways? If we are involved in the rigors of church planting, we need to be sure to receive from him. How do we do this? God is the primary actor here, but as we will see in the next chapter, it requires intentionality on our part as well.

FOR REFLECTION AND DISCUSSION

1. In what ways have you experienced Elijah Syndrome? What have you found helps you navigate this?

2. How would you rate your current physical, emotional, spiritual, and relational health?

3. What is one thing you can do in each of these areas to better let God care for you?

FURTHER RESOURCES

Adrenaline and Stress by Archibald Hart
The Imperfect Pastor by Zack Eswine
The Flourishing in Ministry Project (FlourishingInMinistry.org)

GROWTH

How Can I Plan for My Own
Spiritual Formation?

*The main thing you will give your congregation
is the person you become.*

DALLAS WILLARD

*And we all, who with unveiled faces reflect the Lord's
glory, are being transformed into his image.*

PAUL THE APOSTLE (2 CORINTHIANS 3:18)

"DO YOU WANT TO KNOW THE MOST IMPORTANT LESSON I
LEARNED?"

I was a brand-new church planter, flanked on either side by two
other young planters, and we had been invited out to breakfast by
Donn Engebretson, our denomination's vice president. It was a crisp
fall morning, perfect for hot coffee and buttery pancakes, but we had
completely forgotten about the food in front of us.

Donn began with some light-hearted self-deprecation, opining
that his own failed attempt at church planting was likely the reason
our tribe decided we needed to start assessing our church planters,

not just throw any willing participant into the role. But he quickly got to the point he hoped to impress on us.

"You know," he began, "before I was in my current role, I spent some years as the head of Ordered Ministry." We knew this department well, as we were all working our way through the ordination process. "In those years I had the joy of seeing a lot of great men and women come into ministry." Don paused. "I also had the pain of walking alongside those pastors who had to surrender their credentials because of a moral failure."

We each sat up a little stiffer. "Every pastor who had an affair, who took money, who developed an addiction to drugs or alcohol or gambling or pornography—I sat with them while they poured out their stories, and wept with them as they lamented what, for some, would be the end of their ministry careers. And you know what? There was one factor that every one of them had in common. Do you want to know the most important lesson I learned, sitting with all of those pastors?"

We were all leaning forward now, barely breathing. Donn continued slowly, accentuating every word: *"Everyone takes care of themselves."*

"There are no exceptions to this rule," he continued. "We would all like to think we can just keep going, giving more and more, taking care of others, week after week, year after year. But in reality, that isn't how it works. Every one of us *has to be* replenished somehow—to do *something* to alleviate being hurt, stressed out, tired, discouraged. And those who don't learn to take care of themselves in healthy ways—a strong spiritual life, good work-life balance, quality time with family and friends—inevitably end up taking care of themselves in unhealthy ways."

Donn paused again to make eye contact with each of us. "The most important thing you can do as young pastors is develop healthy habits and a strong spiritual life."

WHY WE CAN'T AFFORD TO WING IT

Church planters are well known for being nimble and adaptive. Or as my church planting coach was fond of telling me, "Church planting is a lot like building an airplane while it's in the air." You get used to winging it.

But when it comes to our spiritual lives, we can't afford to wing it. We need to be deliberate and thoughtful when it comes to our own spiritual growth. There are three key truths I try to keep in mind that help motivate me toward intentionality in my spiritual formation and prevent me from allowing my spiritual life to slowly devolve into something haphazard.

Truth 1: Church planting is a marathon, not a sprint. Somehow, after a life-long aversion to running, in my mid-thirties I caught the running bug. For a combination of health and ego reasons, I decided I needed to start exercising multiple times a week, and running seemed like the way to go. As an untrained runner, I laced up my shiny new shoes, did some perfunctory stretches, and took off down the sidewalk. In my mind, I imagined myself zipping along for miles, the breeze pushing my hair back, neighborhood dogs and cats jumping out of my path to avoid the speeding comet racing down the street. In reality, I barely made it to the end of the block before I was gasping for air and my pace was reduced to an awkward, lilting trot. I'm pretty sure neighborhood pets looked on, but in pity rather than awe.

Your pace has to match the distance you want to travel.

That day I learned what more seasoned runners already know: *your pace has to match the distance you want to travel.* Strictly speaking, there was nothing wrong with the speed I was going—if I only needed to travel to the end of my street. But if I wanted to run farther, I would need to adjust my pace accordingly.

As church planters, it is crucial that we regularly ask ourselves, *Is my pace sustainable?* Yes, there are seasons in a church's life, including those first harried months of a church's beginning, where we are going to be putting in a ridiculous number of hours in positively erratic ways. But we must come to those seasons cognizant of the fact that such seasons need to be the exception rather than the rule.

Church planting is a marathon, not a sprint. If we want to still be in ministry ten, twenty, fifty years from now, we need to learn to run at a pace that is sustainable.

Truth 2: My health and my church's health are inextricably linked. "Follow my example, as I follow the example of Christ," Paul instructs the church in Corinth (1 Cor 11:1). I've never gotten comfortable enough with this statement to be able to say anything like it to my church, as I more than anyone am aware of the ways I do and don't model Christ well. But I'm learning more and more over time that my church *does* follow my example, whether I like it or not. In fact, after sixteen years, I can safely say that our church's strengths and weaknesses largely mirror my own.

Why is this the case? Our ministry is never just a function of what we do, but of who we are and who we are becoming. Consequently, whatever is in us overflows into those nearest us, and eventually into our congregation as a whole. This is why Paul can instruct Timothy to be diligent, both in the example he sets (v. 12) and in the content of his teaching (v. 13). Read it slowly:

> Don't let anyone look down on you because you are young, but set an example for the believers in speech, in conduct, in love, in faith and in purity. Until I come, devote yourself to the public reading of Scripture, to preaching and to teaching. (1 Tim 4:12-13)

Paul is not merely noting that the church *may* see Timothy's life, but Paul *wants* the church to see Timothy's life and learn from it. Then Paul adds this:

> Be diligent in these matters; give yourself wholly to them, so that *everyone may see your progress*. (1 Tim 4:15)

This is fascinating. That the church will see Timothy's *progress* implies that he is not only to let the church see the example of when he gets things right but of his failings as well. His modeling will not just be of glowing successes but also his stumbles along the way. Too often we only want to let our churches see us when we have it all together, but Paul believes there is value in the church seeing the process, not just the final product. Watching someone grow teaches you how to grow.

In fact, I would assert that the way we live our lives—the Christlike character that we do or don't develop—is going to do more to teach our churches than our preaching ever will. When we are done, our people will remember very few of our sermons. What they are going to primarily remember are the stories we told and the kind of people we were.

Consequently, it is extremely difficult, if not impossible, for a pastor who is unhealthy to have a healthy church. Yes, in the short term, a church may appear healthy. But eventually, over time, that church is going to take on the character of its leaders. So, while a healthy pastor isn't the only thing needed to create a healthy church, I would assert that it is an indispensable ingredient.

"Watch your life *and* your doctrine closely," Paul concludes (1 Tim 4:16). Who we are—the example we set, as well as what we teach—is going to shape those we lead.

This is why we can say with Parker Palmer, "Self-care is never a selfish act—it is simply good stewardship of the only gift I have, the gift I was put on earth to offer to others. Anytime we can listen to true self and give it the care it requires, we do so not only for ourselves, but for the many others whose lives we touch."[1]

Friends, the simple truth is this: unhealthy pastors will grow unhealthy churches. Even if you might not be motivated to pursue intentional spiritual growth for your own sake, consider doing it for the sake of your church.

Truth 3: Training takes you further than trying. Let's go back to my running story. The wrong pacing was only the beginning of my problems. That first fateful day, I guesstimated I was fit enough to run three miles. But even after downshifting my pace to something more appropriate, the picture wasn't pretty. I huffed and puffed my way through about a mile and a half before the world started spinning, and the morning's breakfast threatened to come back up. I began looking around to see which lawn looked softest so I could aim for it when I passed out. And why didn't I bring my cell phone? I wouldn't even be able to tell my wife where to find my body.

Unhealthy pastors will grow unhealthy churches.

Now, picturing me in that sorry state, consider this question: If I had tried really, really hard, could I have run a marathon that day? Clearly not, you wisely say. If your body is shutting down by mile two, you'll never make it anywhere near mile twenty-six. But, we might ask, what if I tried super hard, harder than I had ever tried before? No, you say, trying harder might let you run a little farther, but it won't get you to a marathon distance.

But on the other hand, what if instead of trying to run a full marathon, I gave myself a few days to recover and then dragged myself out to run one mile? And what if I kept getting up day after day and running one mile until I was strong enough to run two? And then, what if as I kept training, I slowly gained enough endurance that I could run three miles? If I kept training, and maybe I ditched the Coca-Cola and started eating some vegetables, could I eventually run five miles? Ten? Eventually, could I run twenty-six? Yes, you might say, if you methodically and consistently trained yourself to run that distance, then it is possible that eventually you could run a marathon. (And this is in fact what happened. With a lot of training I eventually ran the Los Angeles Marathon.)

The lesson is simple enough as it pertains to physical training, but how many of us actually approach our spiritual life this way?

"Train yourself to be godly," Paul says to Ephesus's young pastor, drawing as he often does on an athletic metaphor (1 Tim 4:7). Athletes are strong and fast because they train themselves to be. "Approach your spiritual life in the same way," Paul seems to suggest. "If you want to be godly, then you must not merely try hard to be godly. Like the athlete competing for the prize (cf. 1 Cor 9:24-27), you must methodically and intentionally arrange your life in such a way that you are prepared for the arena once you get there."

Jesus, too, speaking to his disciples, tells them that every student "who is fully trained will be like their master" (Lk 6:40). To apprentice ourselves to Jesus is to train ourselves to live our lives as he would live them.

Yet many of us, rather than training for godliness, simply try harder. It is worth pausing to consider: Will we, by trying harder, be able to bless that person who moves on to another church after we invested so much in them? To forgive that congregant who misrepresents us and does harm to our good name? To be patient with the person who perpetually finds something to criticize?

Not likely. It's only in training ourselves to be godly that we will slowly develop sufficient maturity to think, feel, and act like Jesus in those moments. As Dallas Willard has put it, "We learn that we cannot do what we should do just by trying, but that through training, in time, we can become the kind of person who would do the good with little thought or effort."[2]

Physically or spiritually, trying harder gets us more of what we are currently getting. Training, on the other hand, enables us to do what we cannot currently do by merely trying.[3]

It's only in training ourselves to be godly that we will slowly develop sufficient maturity to think, feel, and act like Jesus.

And how do we do this? How do we train for godliness? This is where the spiritual disciplines come in. The historical church has developed a tremendous tool to help us to move from haphazard spirituality to intentionality in our spiritual formation. It's called a rule of life.

A PLAN FOR OUR SPIRITUAL FORMATION

The idea of a rule of life as a spiritual discipline gets its origin in the early monastic movement.

In the early centuries of the church, if you were to enter a monastic order, you would come under that monastery's rule. The rule would instruct you in everything from your times of prayer to how you were to relate to your fellow monks, all with the intent that the rule would lend structure to your spiritual growth. In describing its function, the monks frequently invoked the image of a trellis. A trellis is a tool that helps a young vine get off the ground and find stability as it grows, allowing it to be maximally healthy and fruitful.

Think of your rule of life as your personal plan for spiritual formation. It consists of those practices, relationships, and experiences you believe God is leading you into for you to grow as an apprentice of Jesus. Many find utilizing the rule as a spiritual discipline to be very helpful in bringing one's spiritual life from haphazard to intentional.[4]

I've included my rule (in its current state; it's always evolving) in a sidebar as a point of reference and to show what this looks like for me.[5] (I place this here not for you to copy, but hopefully to spur your thinking for what your own should look like.)

When putting together a rule, here are a few things to keep in mind.

TIM'S RULE OF LIFE

- Set aside twenty to forty minutes each morning for solitude, prayer, and Scripture.
- Take a monthly day of solitude and a twenty-four-hour solo retreat annually.

- Practice the presence of God daily.
- Observe the Sabbath (worship, rest, play with people I love) weekly. Limit ministry nights to one or two per week, with a maximum of three.
- Meet weekly with spiritual friends for confession, prayer, and accountability.
- Meet monthly with a spiritual director or mentor.
- Regularly read good books.
- Eat dinner with my family five times per week, keep a weekly date night with my wife, and find at least one time each month to play with friends.
- Exercise four to five times per week.
- Serve the poor monthly.

Be realistic. Commit to what you can do, not to what you think you should do. Take into account your season of life with the benefits and limitations this season brings, your current state of spiritual fitness, and plan accordingly.

Sometimes a person will come to me, feeling inspired to be more intentional about their spiritual growth, and say something like, "I'm going to commit to an hour of prayer every day!"

"How much do you pray now?" is typically my first question. If the answer is "barely at all," I encourage them to abandon their prescribed hour and instead commit to five minutes a day.

Why? I've seen this story enough times to know that the person who commits to a goal that far outside their current capabilities will likely be so discouraged by the end of the week that they will quit altogether. They become like the proverbial runner who sets out to run a marathon when they can't yet run two miles.

The person who commits to more than they can realistically accomplish often ends up discouraged and guilt-ridden and abandons their rule. Better to be realistic about where you are, start there without guilt or shame, and slowly increase as you develop more spiritual stamina.

An important corollary to this is that we need to allow our rule to be flexible enough that we can add, subtract, and adjust practices guilt-free. My rule is ever a work in process. When I first began the discipline of keeping a rule, it only included a few items. Over time, as I've grown, it has grown. As I slowly mature in Christ, I find that I need more practices, not fewer. This is because as time goes on, I discover more of what I need in order to grow well. I also learn what I don't need that I thought I needed, and I take those off my rule.

I also find that certain seasons of life, as well as the ups and downs in certain seasons of ministry, call for adjustments to my rule. For instance, in sleepless seasons, like when our children were babies, or when I was traveling more for ministry, I found I was drawn to the comfort and stability of fixed-hour prayer, with its structured readings and prayers at intervals throughout the day.[6] And in seasons of ministry where I am feeling beat up or scared of failure, I find I'm drawn to journaling my prayers and praying the Psalms. Whatever the reason, we need to feel freedom to adjust our rule as our circumstances change, and with sensitivity to what the Holy Spirit might be wanting to work in us at any given time.

Be balanced. We might be tempted to make our rule entirely of those practices which come most naturally to us. And indeed, because God has wired us to connect with him in particular ways, most of our rule should reflect that reality. But at the same time, we want to be sure our rule reflects a balance of disciplines that come naturally to us as well as those which may be more stretching.

God has wired me in such a way that I tend to best meet him in what Gary Thomas would call the contemplative and intellectual pathways.[7] Consequently, practices like solitude, prayer, and meditation on Scripture are like my lifeblood. If I don't incorporate these into my life in regular, significant ways, I quickly wither.

Yet, important as these solitary disciplines are, I have to remind myself to balance them with more communal disciplines as well—meeting with spiritual friends for fellowship, accountability, and play. While I don't feel the need for these as readily as I do my solo disciplines, they are vitally important to my spiritual growth as well. Without the balance they bring, I will be spiritually misshapen.

Others are wired differently, and so balance will look different for them. One friend is extroverted to the point of being the human equivalent of a golden retriever. He would never need to remind himself to be part of a small group, as talking with others about what God is doing is where he most naturally connects with God. Yet he has to discipline himself to pursue some of the more solitary disciplines. While these are not as natural to his personality, he recognizes that he needs these, too, if he is going to grow properly.

As important as it is to practice disciplines that your soul craves and that resonate with you, we also do well to practice disciplines that might not be as natural to us but will help in developing areas of need. For instance, a person wanting to grow in humility might practice the discipline of secrecy, the person struggling with gossip or sins involving speech might benefit from practicing the discipline of silence, and spiritual directors have long prescribed fasting to the person struggling with lust or otherwise wanting to develop self-control.[8]

I also meet God when my mind is stimulated by new thinking, so to grow I need to be sure I am making time to read good books. There are other practices, like fasting (which teaches me to deny my body's appetites) and serving those less fortunate (which keeps my heart tender), which I am less likely to be drawn to but that I need if I am to grow properly in Christ.

In addition to balance in which practices we choose, it is important to think about balance in terms of how often certain disciplines occur. For me, practices like praying, reading Scripture, and practicing God's presence need to be part of my daily rhythm. When I miss these, it's like I've missed a meal. Others, like sabbath-keeping, happen on a weekly basis, and still other practices work best for me if I practice them monthly (like a day of solitude) or yearly (like an overnight prayer retreat).

The context is grace. Finally, we need to be careful to let our rule be a guide and a friend, not a law or a taskmaster. For many of us, it is easy to let our spiritual disciplines take on an oughtness that puts them on par with a command from Scripture. Consequently, when we fail to live out everything in our rule, we experience guilt and shame as if we have sinned or somehow let God down.

But this is neither the character of a rule of life nor its intention! Like a trellis, our rule is there to provide support and structure so we might grow well. When you fail to live out a part of your rule, don't roll it up like a newspaper and use it to beat yourself. You haven't sinned. Dust yourself off, and in Christ's strength, try again tomorrow. Embrace the fact that you are weak and need God's grace to strengthen you.

And if over time you find you cannot live out some aspect of your rule, change it. Recognize that there will be some practices you are drawn to but are not yet ready to regularly do. Start where you are, and as you grow, consider making these practices longer or more frequent. Recognize too that there will be days, weeks, and whole seasons where you don't keep your rule very well. That's okay. God's grace is sufficient for that too.

Grace, after all, is not just for when we fall short. It is the ongoing gift of God to make us like his Son, Jesus. As Dallas Willard reminds us, "If we—through well-directed and unrelenting action— effectually receive the grace of God in salvation and transformation, we certainly will be incrementally changed toward inward Christlikeness. The transformation of our outer life, especially of our behavior, will follow suit."[9]

Let's get after it.

FOR REFLECTION AND DISCUSSION

As you put together your rule of life, here are a few questions to guide you.

1. What disciplines are best suited to the natural ways God has made you to connect with him? What disciplines may be less natural, but address specific areas of need, sin areas, or harmful internal scripts?

2. Which disciplines do you need to practice daily? Weekly? Monthly? Yearly? When and where will these take place?

3. Does your rule include both solo and communal disciplines?

4. What changes do you need to make to your schedule in order to make your rule a reality? How will following your rule impact others in your life? What conversations do you need to have with them?

5. Is there a friend, mentor, or coach you can share this with for counsel and accountability?

FURTHER RESOURCES

Sacred Rhythms by Ruth Haley Barton
The Spirit of the Disciplines by Dallas Willard
The Common Rule by Justin Whitmel Earley

3

SUFFERING

Can I Embrace a Life Peppered
with Difficulty?

*God gives us the vision, then he takes us into the valley
to batter us into the shape of the vision. It is in the
valley that so many of us faint and give way.*

OSWALD CHAMBERS

Conflicts on the outside, fears within.

PAUL THE APOSTLE (2 CORINTHIANS 7:5)

"YOU WILL BE BROKEN."

I was sitting in a church gymnasium on a rainy Seattle morning when I first heard those words—the first words an aspiring church planter hears in our denomination's church-planter training. In the years to come, I would repeat these words to myself countless times as I experienced their truth. Years later I would repeat them to others when I was one of the teachers of this class.

The church planter's life is full of exhilarating highs. Baptizing that person you never thought would receive Christ, seeing a marriage make it that you were certain would crash and burn, witnessing in ways big and small God's kingdom come and his will be done in your city.

The planter's life is also full of pain. Heartbreaking betrayals, that loyal ally that you thought would always be with you leaving the church, fatigue, failures both big and small, maybe burnout, or even the church's closure.

You will be broken.

It isn't a matter of if, but when. If you are a church planter, it's going to hurt.

In fact, if there is any one reality that led to the writing of this book, it is this: suffering is inevitable, and when it appears, it is going to reveal parts of us that are in need of healing, formation, and correction.

What I've seen undermine church planters most often is not a lack of skill, spiritual gifting, zeal, or drive. Most often, it's an underdeveloped spiritual life. And nothing reveals this like suffering.

What do you do when your spouse says they can no longer do it, that they can't keep going? When that trusted mentor or best friend quits the church? When your church seems to be hemorrhaging people, money, or enthusiasm? What do you do on those nights when you lie awake, wondering if maybe you misheard God's call and should never have started this venture in the first place?

> *Suffering is going to reveal parts of us that are in need of healing, formation, and correction.*

You don't fix these things by attending another seminar, taking a refresher course on preaching, developing a better outreach strategy, or reading another book on how to be a catalytic leader. No, the only refuge against the brokenness that inevitably results from planting is a heart, soul, mind, and body that are immersed in the presence of Jesus.

HOW FRUIT HAPPENS

None of us enjoys being in the pain cave, and our automatic response when we encounter suffering is to alleviate it as quickly as possible. But consider this: What if suffering is part of how God means to make you a fruitful pastor? What if the most important thing we can do in suffering is not to alleviate it, but to meet God in the midst of it? To let the suffering be part of our formation?

This morning a planter I coach sent me this text: "This church planting process is bringing me to my knees. Really making me think about how much I really trust Jesus and how much I really know him."

I fired off this reply, and for the rest of the day have been reflecting on its truth: "Sounds about right! Sometimes I think being a planter is more about what God is doing in me than what he's doing through me."

A friend was recently telling me about a trip to Napa Valley. They knew a big wig with one of the area's wine producers, and as a result he and his wife were invited to tour the caverns under the vineyard where the wine was stored as it fermented and to hear from a master vintner about the process for producing good wine. "Step one is getting the best juice from your grapes," the vintner explained. "To do this, during certain times in the vine's life, we go for long stretches without watering it." *What?* my friend thought. *How does starving the vine for something as essential as water lead to better grapes?* The vintner went on: "It's counterintuitive until you realize that developing the best fruit isn't about the season immediately in front of you—it's about the long-term vitality of the vine. Starving the vine forces it to put its roots deeper into the earth in search of water. And ultimately it's the vine with the deepest roots that produces the best fruit."

My friend's mind flashed to the words of Jesus: "I am the vine; you are the branches. If you remain in me and I in you, you will bear much fruit; apart from me you can do nothing" (Jn 15:5).

None of us likes the inevitable suffering that comes with our vocation. But is it possible that such seasons are God's invitation to put our roots deeper? That suffering may even be *necessary* for a life of lasting fruit?

Paul alludes to this in Romans 5, where he asserts that we are right to "glory in our sufferings, because we know that suffering produces perseverance; perseverance, character; and character, hope" (Rom 5:3-5).

None of us likes to suffer, yet at the same time, I can't imagine anyone having a fruitful church plant if they don't have perseverance, character, and hope—traits that come as a result of suffering. It seems that suffering contains within it the seeds of our success.

TROUBLES OUTSIDE, FEARS INSIDE

I have found Paul's second letter to the Corinthians particularly helpful in recognizing these seeds, as this may be his most vulnerable telling of his own ministry pains. These words sum up his experience: "When we came to Macedonia, we had no rest, but we were harassed at every turn—*conflicts on the outside, fears within*" (2 Cor 7:5).

> *Suffering contains within it the seeds of our success.*

I relate to this on so many levels. There are always conflicts on the outside—the pressures of fires to put out, budgets that look shaky, opposition from community leaders who may not value the church's presence, scorn from those too enlightened or self-sufficient to embrace religion.

We know from this letter that when Paul says conflicts on the outside, he means outside himself, not outside the church. These same people of whom Paul can say, "You have such a place in our hearts that we would live or die with you" (v. 3), are the source of much of his pain! They will be for you and me as well.

I'm writing this chapter the morning after a long leadership meeting, called on short notice to deal with the latest turn in a sticky church discipline issue. The situation has been going on for three very long years, and it's been nasty. Personal attacks against me, my wife, and most of our leaders; threats of litigation; attempts to sour other church members toward the church or me or both. It's been exhausting, and it shows no signs of stopping. And as is so often the case, this comes not from one on the fringes, but a congregant who has spent many meals at our table and shared their heart while sitting on our couch—one we counted as a friend.

I went to bed last night reminded that this wasn't our first bout of friendly fire, and it won't be out last. Flannery O'Connor poignantly wrote of the pastor's role, "You have to suffer as much from the church as for it. . . . The only thing that makes the church endurable is that somehow it is the body of Christ, and on this we are fed."[1]

But perhaps worse than the conflicts on the outside are the "fears within"—those gnawing doubts we hear when the rush of the moment is over, and we lie in our beds waiting for sleep. *Did I mishear my calling? Do I actually have what it takes to make this thing happen? I don't know what I'm doing. I feel like a fraud.*

Yet here is the remarkable thing about Paul. Even in the midst of these exterior and interior sources of suffering, he finds real joy and comfort in the midst of the rigors of rearing this unruly young church. In the verses that follow, Paul receives an unexpected gift in the form of good news from a beloved visitor, and his next lines are shot through with joy: "But God [I love those two words], who comforts the downcast, comforted us . . . now I am happy . . . by this we are all encouraged . . . we were especially delighted . . ." (vv. 6-13).

How do we do this? When we find ourselves in a place of suffering, how do we fight off despair and continue to minister from a place of joy? What practices, attitudes, and perspectives can help us drive our roots deeper into Jesus? Three in particular stand out to me from Paul's discourse with his nettlesome church in Corinth.

Humility. Far be it from me to suggest that as church planters we may need to grow in humility, but . . . as church planters, we may need to grow in humility. If you will permit me a broad generalization, church planters often come as an odd mixture of overconfidence and self-doubt. Maybe it has to do with the strength of the spiritual gifts they possess, the heady response one gets to looking behind you and seeing others actually following, or the reality that anyone who sets out to do this has to be just a little bit crazy. If you don't identify with this, please take no offense, and just ignore me.

But if perhaps you can see some bit of yourself in this description, take comfort in knowing you aren't the first.

In 2 Corinthians 12, Paul shares about an ongoing difficulty he was faced with, what he terms "a thorn in my flesh, a messenger of Satan, to torment me" (2 Cor 12:7). Why, we might ask, did God give Paul this gift of the thorn, and decline to take it away when asked? It was, Paul says, "to keep me from becoming conceited" (v. 7). Apparently, Paul the church planter could get a little cocky too.

Suffering keeps me humble because it teaches me things about myself that I'd rather not know.

Not too long ago, a parent, misunderstanding a situation, wrote a pretty nasty email to our children's pastor. The pastor was brand-new on staff, and reeling from the email, wasn't quite sure what to do. "You don't have to do anything," I told him. "I need to be the one to handle this." I called the parent and asked, "Can you help me understand why you wrote this?" We proceeded to have a courteous but fairly uncomfortable conversation, with me explaining, "We don't treat each other this way at Life, and if you are going to be part of this body, I need you to handle your grievances differently."

Now, you also have to understand, if you were to ask what drains me most in ministry, I would answer without hesitation that it's when people leave the church. I'm sort of like a big golden retriever who gets attached quickly, so it tears me up when people leave. Consequently, I'm learning, I have a tendency to tolerate bad behavior longer than I should. But in this situation, and previous ones like it, I have no problem establishing a boundary that may well cause someone to opt out of the church.

But here is where the uncomfortable lesson comes in. Not too long after this incident, someone wrote a nasty email to me. Several, actually, and our face-to-face follow ups were not much better. But in this situation, rather than gently and firmly establishing a boundary as I have for our children's pastor and other leaders at Life when they are taking fire, I just continued to take it. One of our leaders sagely pointed out the contrast. "You would never let that person speak to me the way they are speaking to you. Why do you think that is?"

I just stood there, dumbstruck. Not only did I have no answer, I didn't even realize that is what I was doing. But as soon as they said it, I realized this wasn't the first time. This pattern had developed in my blind spot, and I had no idea it was even there.

Their question resulted in some uncomfortable soul searching as I tried to honestly explore my internal monologue around this. I heard my inner voice saying things like, *It's okay, I can take it.* Do I think that because I am the pastor, I have to be stronger than others? *It's more important that they not leave the church.* If they do leave the church, do I think I've failed them? *But if they aren't here, I can't shepherd them and help them grow past this.* Do I not think it possible that if they do huff off and leave, God will use even that to teach them something they need to learn? Or do I believe I'm indispensable to God's plan? That he can't call someone else to come alongside if they decide to leave me?

We fear suffering, but I wonder if we would do better to fear its absence. Without episodes of pain exposing our weaknesses, we would remain vulnerable to all manner of unhealth, which God in his grace wants to free us from.

In times of suffering, can we be people who humbly ask God, "Are their areas of my life that you want to expose through this? Places where I need healing, correction, or even rebuke?" Can we go even further, and humbly ask trusted spiritual friends to tell us what they see as well?

Dependency. One of my church planting mentors, Dave Olson, likes to say, "Most of your ministry fruit will come from your strengths. But don't forget that your weaknesses can get you fired."[2] We each need to be able to recognize, own, and mitigate our areas of weakness.

But is it possible that God wants to use our weaknesses to produce fruit too? What if your weaknesses are more than just inconveniences to be removed, but the very things God wants to use? I hear Jesus saying something like this to Paul in 2 Corinthians 12: "Three times I pleaded with God to take [the thorn] away from me. But he said to me, '*My grace is sufficient for you, for my power is made perfect in weakness*'" (2 Cor 12:8-9).

How can it be that Paul's greatest asset might be his weakness rather than his strength? Could that be the case for you and me too?

Here is how I see this work out in my life. When I first began in ministry, I prayed hard because I was desperate. I didn't have a lot of natural gifting, and I knew it. If God didn't show up, I was in big trouble. But over time, as he has developed my competence in certain areas, I am not as desperate. I can perform competently, and consequently it's easier for me to be nonchalant about remaining attached to the vine. Or, to put it another way, I'm learning that I don't always trust God for what I can do by myself.

But then a bout of suffering comes along, grabs us by the scruff of the neck, and shakes us back into reality: I cannot by my own effort work lasting spiritual change in anybody. Suffering exposes the weaknesses we've kept hidden behind our carefully constructed façades and awakens us to our need to depend on Jesus' power, not our own.

I am, whether I am cognizant of it or not, entirely dependent on God's power graciously making itself known through me. Without suffering, I would not experience the greatest fruitfulness, because I would not live in dependency on Christ's power. This is why Paul can truthfully say, "When I am weak, *then* I am strong" (2 Cor 12:10).

And this, to me, is where Paul gets really interesting. Rather than responding to his weaknesses in the way that I typically do, by trying to expunge those weaknesses he can and conceal those he can't, he embraces them. "I boast gladly about my weaknesses," he says, "so that Christ's power might rest on me. . . . That is why, for Christ's sake,

I delight in weaknesses, in insults, in hardships, in persecutions, in difficulties. For when I am weak, *then* I am strong" (vv. 9-10).

I find that Paul's counterintuitive practice is one that we as church planters do well to emulate. Rather than running from suffering, he *delights* in it. He embraces it, even boasts about it. Not out of masochism, but out of genuine faith that hardship means God is working something good in him. And this means good for others as well.

The pain of pruning doesn't come to slacking believers as punishment for their laziness, but as a gift to the fruitful that they might bear even more fruit.

Some of our sufferings are the results of our own mistakes or blind spots, and others are the result of other people's sin or poor choices. And at yet other times our suffering seems to just be a general result of living in a fallen world. But ultimately, I'm not sure the source of the suffering matters. In all of it, like the good parent that he is, God stands ready to seize the opportunity to do whatever work is needed in us at that time.

I believe Jesus was getting at this same dynamic when he said, "Every branch that does bear fruit he prunes so that it will be even more fruitful" (Jn 15:2). The pain of pruning doesn't come to slacking believers as punishment for their laziness, but as a gift to the fruitful that they might bear even more fruit. Paul knows this, and it reframes his entire experience of suffering.

What about you, friend? Are you able to embrace hardship as a gift, as pruning? To give thanks for your weaknesses and your sufferings, as they will allow God's power to better flow through you?

Empathy. Paul is notable for his resilience and positivity in the midst of suffering. But it is also noteworthy that the one thing Paul doesn't do is *deny* his pain. Consider the following:

We do not want you to be uninformed, brothers and sisters, about the troubles we experienced in the province of Asia. We were under great pressure, far beyond our ability to endure, so that we despaired of life itself. (2 Cor 1:8)

I wrote you out of great distress and anguish of heart and with many tears. (2 Cor 2:4)

Five times I received from the Jews the forty lashes minus one. Three times I was beaten with rods, once I was pelted with stones, three times I was shipwrecked, I spent a night and a day in the open sea, I have been constantly on the move. I have been in danger from rivers, in danger from bandits, in danger from my fellow Jews, in danger from Gentiles; in danger in the city, in danger in the country, in danger at sea; and in danger from false believers. I have labored and toiled and have often gone without sleep; I have known hunger and thirst and have often gone without food; I have been cold and naked. Besides everything else, I face daily the pressure of my concern for all the churches. Who is weak, and I do not feel weak? Who is led into sin, and I do not inwardly burn? (2 Cor 11:24-29)

His is not the short-term relief that comes from pretending things are alright when they really are not. Rather, Paul is forthright about naming just how painful his experience is. And only *after* naming the pain does he place his suffering in proper perspective in light of eternity.

As I read these statements, I flash back to one of Paul's opening statements in this epistle:

Praise be to the God and Father of our Lord Jesus Christ, the Father of compassion and the God of all comfort, who comforts us in all our troubles, so that we can comfort those in any trouble with the comfort we ourselves receive from God. (2 Cor 1:3-4)

Here Paul notes another positive fruit that can come out of suffering: empathy. In what has been called the circle of comfort, Paul's suffering leads him to experience the Father's compassion and comfort, which he is then able to turn around and offer to others. Without suffering, where would we develop the empathy needed to care for hurting people well? How would we be able to meet people in their pain in a genuine way?

When we started Life Cov, Samantha and I were nearly five years deep into an excruciating journey of unsuccessful attempts to have children. The pain of failing month after month to get pregnant, multiple doctors who poked and prodded but ultimately remained perplexed as to the source of our infertility, and three miscarriages to match the elation of the three times we had gotten pregnant. We were done—emotionally and physically spent—and all we wanted to do was curl up in our pain and shut everyone else out.

But then, here we were, starting a church where we longed for people to live deeply and authentically with one another. How would this happen if we ourselves weren't willing to invite others into our pain? Slowly but deliberately, fueled by large doses of God's grace, we let others enter our pain. And as hard as it was, God's comfort was mediated to us through others who wept with us, prayed for us, and carried us. And then, these same dear saints were able to share in our joy when our first beautiful baby made her way into the world.

But what's more, God used our pain greatly for others. Not only did our example help set the DNA for how our church would care for one another, but it better equipped Samantha and me to be a source of comfort for others—in general, and in infertility in particular. For the next five years God seemed to bring us a steady stream of young couples who were experiencing infertility and loss. And we were able to comfort them with the comfort God had graced upon us.

"Our service will not be perceived as authentic," Henri Nouwen warns, "unless it comes from a heart wounded by the suffering about which we speak. Thus, nothing can be written about ministry without a deeper understanding of the ways in which ministers can make their own wounds available as a source of healing . . . When our wounds cease to be a source of shame, and become a source of healing, we have become wounded healers."[3]

We see in Paul's honesty echoes of the Jewish practice of lament— a practice I believe is crucial for us as church planters. To church plant is to experience so much loss—people who move away, or leave you for the nearest megachurch, or die, or who were once present but are now lost in the busyness of life. The relational loss alone can be crippling. Some experts estimate that the norm is for half of a new church's launch team to leave in the first year.[4]

Therefore, as planters we have to take time to lament. To come face to face with our pain, name it, acknowledge that it hurts, and take time to grieve.

I'm not very good at this practice. Most often, my first response to pain is to move quickly past it, thinking I'm fine. But inevitably it comes out later, most often in disproportional emotion expressed in another area. I'll catch myself being curt and irritable with my wife or kids, or getting way too angry about how someone is driving, or making too much about a situation that should be small, and think, *Wait a minute—this isn't actually about them. It's about me being hurt, or scared, or sad.* This is a telltale sign for me that there may be an ungrieved loss I need to process.

I have found two practical helps as I learn to lament. The first is praying the Psalms, particularly those that express pain or cry out for God's comfort. They provide me with the words I can't seem to find on my own—words that help me ferret out and express my own pain to God. So I pray them. I *enter* these Psalms, pausing after each line to make the psalmists' prayers my own, adding the details of my situation to theirs.

The second is running. Stress, sorrow, anger—all these create a physiological response as well as an emotional one. We physically hold our sorrow in our bodies, and exercise helps us release the tension that builds up in our tissues. Running, walking, yoga, weightlifting—as well as body work like massage or chiropractic adjustments—help us address the bodily dimension of grief.

Whatever helps you grieve, lean into it. Church planting is a life of loss. We have to anticipate that going in, and find ways to invite Jesus into our pain.

JOEL SEYMOUR, SENIOR PASTOR,
LANCASTER VINEYARD, LANCASTER, OHIO

At age thirty-four I was an overweight and overworked pastor with a constant tightness in the center of my chest. I stumbled into a seminary for a series of retreats led by Dr. Terry Wardle. It was there I learned to lament. My ungrieved losses, both in planting and in life, led me to self-medicate with more church activity and too much food. Neither were forming me into a spiritually healthy person, let alone a spiritually healthy pastor. And neither helped me truly deal with loss.

Loss. It's built into church planting. Even when a planter experiences something positive—like multiplying groups and adding a public service—there is loss. This shouldn't surprise us, as the very act of planting a church involves loss as we leave our home, our town, and our sending church (as well as relational intimacy with those we leave behind). Of course, as Tim points out in this chapter, even more painful losses await the planter.

Ungrieved losses leave planters susceptible to emotional stuffing, hard-heartedness, and prone to seek relief in empty wells (Jer 2:13). I should know, as I was eight years into my *second* church plant before stumbling into Dr. Wardle's retreat and learning how to lament.

Dr. Wardle taught that we should model our lamenting after Jesus' lament in the Garden of Gethsemane. Jesus' lament took place before his Father, in a safe place, without censoring, in the presence of the Spirit, and with the prayerful support of his friends (the disciples). We can use this as the framework for our lament as well.

What does lament look like? Let me suggest two practices that I have found helpful. First, write laments when you experience deep loss. These letters are to be written to the heavenly Father in raw, earthy language expressing your loss. While your words will undoubtedly include a palette of emotions like anger, fear, discouragement, and disillusionment, most find that (like Jesus and the Psalms) these laments eventually turn to praise. After the letter is written, spend time reading it aloud to God, sensing that your Father is present. If you are processing an unusually painful loss, consider inviting a trusted friend to prayerfully listen in as you read it.

Another way I lament is to pray Lamentations 3:17-26, making Jeremiah's words my own. During one particularly hard stretch, I prayed this passage so often I committed it to memory. Jeremiah is safe enough to hurl his uncensored complaint against God. But notice that once he gets his grief "up and out," he is able to praise God and quietly wait on salvation. If you struggle to write a lament, then consider paraphrasing Jeremiah's lament and make it your own.

When should a planter lament? Any time he or she suffers loss. All losses deserve an appropriate level of grief. Of course this can be as simple as acknowledging small losses as they happen. Or it can be as purposeful as writing a lament and asking a friend to help you process.

Loss is built into the church planter's life. But there is much to gain in lamenting: emotional health, becoming a more spiritually formed planter, and most of all, deeper intimacy with your heavenly Father.

Last year I had to say goodbye to a really great church member, and not for the reasons one would hope. He and his family were leaving, he told me, because of an area of theology where we differed. There was plenty of affection between us, and he and I were both hopeful we could navigate this such that they could stay, but it wasn't to be.

This guy and his then-fiancée were with us from literally the very first day of the church. I baptized him as a new believer, married him and his wife, blessed their children in the hospital when they were born, and dedicated them in the church when they were a bit older. They were great servants and faithful givers, and they loved people well. What's more, I don't know if anyone has ever appreciated my teaching more (which feels nice). He would listen attentively on Sunday, taking notes, then listen again to the podcast during the week, sometimes more than once. He asked thoughtful, perceptive questions, and worked hard to apply the Word to his life.

When we met to make the parting official, we both shed tears—he as we sat there over coffee, me in the car after. In the days following, I emailed him and his wife a blessing, apologized for any ways I may have wronged them in all this, and—taking a little risk—offered my top three picks for churches where I thought their family might thrive.

Sometime later I emailed to check in. How is the family holding up? Have you found a new church yet?

His reply simultaneously put on a smile on my lips and a lump in my throat. They had visited a few churches, but none seemed right. Then he went back to the list I gave him. He wrote, "As far as churches go, a good friend of mine recommended a church I had never heard of. . . . Thanks man for helping even in this process. This is the first church since Life that we both felt we could call 'home,' which is exactly what we had been praying for."

"A good friend . . . Thanks man for helping even in this."

The God who comforts us in all our troubles had brought comfort to both him and to me.

FOR REFLECTION AND DISCUSSION

1. The author notes that people leaving the church is the thing that drains him most in ministry. What do you find drains you?

2. Suffering keeps us humble because it teaches us things about ourselves we would rather not know. What has God used suffering to reveal in you that you are now grateful for?

3. Can you think of particular times of suffering that have made you a better "wounded healer"? In what ways have you seen this play out?

FURTHER RESOURCES

Leading with a Limp by Dan Allender
The Emotionally Healthy Leader by Peter Scazzero
The Wounded Healer by Henri Nouwen

4

POWER

Do Others Experience Me as a Safe Person?

Jesus is looking for people he can trust with power.

Dallas Willard

You know that the rulers in this world lord it over their people, and officials flaunt their authority over those under them. But among you it will be different.

Jesus (Mark 10:42-43 NLT)

"Is this person a wounded healer or a healing wounder?" It was one of Don's go-to questions. At the time Don was probably the longest-serving member of the Evangelical Covenant Church's assessment team, having been a regional church planting director for many years in the notoriously difficult Pacific Northwest. I was the team's rookie.

I couldn't help but notice the difference between the questions he would ask and the questions I would ask. I was thinking primarily about the assessee's charisma, their public presence, their ability to gather and retain people. Don was wondering what was happening in the deeper levels of their soul. Whenever he spoke, something in my spirit told me to be quiet and pay attention.

I learned quickly that it was pretty much a given that church planters were wounded. I knew I was, and I found that just about everyone else who came through assessment was too. Some saw this as a liability, but Don saw it as an asset—or at least a potential asset.

If a person had experienced God's grace in the midst of their wounds and was finding depth and maturity as a result, they could be a powerful, empathetic source of healing in the lives of others. They could be, in Henri Nouwen's iconic phrase, a "wounded healer." Or as the apostle Paul put it, they could be leaders who "comfort those in any trouble with the comfort we ourselves receive from God" (2 Cor 1:4).

But what of those who weren't yet healed enough to be of benefit to others? When entrusted with power, these were not wounded healers but too often became what Don termed "healing wounders." When they found themselves in a position of power, their own wounds would cause them to consciously or unconsciously use those around them to meet the needs of their own egos. These leaders were not at a place where we could responsibly entrust them with vulnerable people. Don summed all this up in his frequently posed question: "Is this person a wounded healer, or a healing wounder?"

For any of us in ministry, but perhaps especially for those of us who plant churches, one of the questions we need to ask ourselves is this: *Am I becoming a person who can be trusted with power?*

DO YOU KNOW YOU HAVE POWER?
DO YOU KNOW HOW TO USE IT?

The first few days of our church plant, I struggled with a gnawing discomfort that I couldn't quite put my finger on. Yes, I was nervous about whether or not this church would actually work, but a new concern was stirring as well. A few days earlier I had stood in my living room, sharing the vision of the church I believed God was calling us to plant. And one of the most striking aspects of that experience had been the realization of how much trust people were prepared to place in me. I was an odd mix of confidence and insecurity, so it surprised me how little pushback there was on the crazy dreams I was laying out before the group. I think I half expected someone to stand up and shout, "Are you serious?" then turn to the others and shout, "This guy is a nut!" But all I was getting were questions like "What do we do now?" and "When can we start?" even from those twenty years my senior.

I was suddenly aware of my own power, and it scared me.

In his book *The Challenge of the Disciplined Life: Christian Reflections on Money, Sex, and Power*, Richard Foster advances a sobering thesis. Money, sex, and power, he says, have traditionally been seen as the three core temptations that all believers, and especially Christian leaders, face. In the modern church, he says, when a leader commits a sin that involves sex or money, the consequences are typically swift and devastating. The pastor who has an affair or takes the church's money is almost certainly out of a job, and their ministry may well be over. Their sin is seen as serious, and likely disqualifying for one who aspires to high levels of leadership.

But not so with sins of power, says Foster. Frequently, the pastor who abuses their power is not faced with discipline, but may in fact be rewarded with *more power!* A pastor who is angry or demeaning, who manipulates or uses people, too often is not seen as sinning but is seen as a *strong leader.* So rather than being confronted for their behavior, they are advanced—rewarded with bigger churches and more prestige, and praised for their effectiveness in building the enterprise.[1]

Similarly, Eugene Peterson warns that while today's pastors are sufficiently wary of the intoxicating effect of sex and alcohol, they are all but unaware of the intoxicating effect of crowds. He comments, "Being a pastor is a precarious position, because . . . being a pastor automatically puts you in a position of power; you don't have to do anything to get it. We don't realize how people treat us. And gradually it kind of seeps into our bloodstream, and without even making decisions, it feels good. . . . It becomes addictive. I think power is a very addictive thing, and we're just sitting ducks for it."[2]

Being aware of this dynamic is important for any pastor, but perhaps more so with a church planter because there are fewer checks on our power.

In an established church, there are natural checks on a pastor's power. The new pastor of an established church steps into an existing leadership structure. Formal leaders—boards, elders, deacons—as well as those untitled individuals who are a church's thought-leaders and gatekeepers provide checks on a pastor's power, even in a polity where the pastor is given a high degree of autonomous authority.

Not all planters have denominational authorities over them—a bishop, presbytery, or superintendent. But even if they do, these figures do not have a relational history with the church itself, only with the pastor. So their knowledge of and influence over the church is almost always mediated through pastors, who are unlikely to see or report their own misuses of power.

Even a church's history serves as a check on a pastor's power. An established church can look at previous pastors and have some semblance of what a pastor should do and how he or she should behave. Frustrating as it is for pastors to lead change in a church with an established way of doing things, the fact that there is a "way we've always done it" gives a congregation a baseline for what is and isn't appropriate, and empowers a church to speak up if something seems off. In a church plant, there is no such history.

THE POWER OF A PASTOR'S WORDS

As a pastor, I'm always surprised at the power my words have to bring either healing or harm. When we are really listening to the Holy Spirit and to the person in front of us, there are times when we speak a word of grace with the quiet forcefulness of conviction and are amazed to find that word is powerful enough to break years-long bondages or to heal life-long wounds. And the reverse is also true. A careless or angry word can hit like a baseball bat, embittering a person toward God or the church for years to come.

I'm always surprised at the power my words have to bring either healing or harm.

Two incidents stay with me, even years later. One was with a young worship leader. He was trying to get his feet wet in worship leading, and we were butting heads on how things should be done. I asked him to do one thing, and he did another. I misunderstood his actions as defiance, when in fact he was just young and excited to stretch his creative wings. I took him aside and confronted him. My demeanor was condescending and accusing, assuming the worst of his motives. He felt attacked, lost his temper, and stormed out. Though words of apology and forgiveness were shared in the following days, the relationship was permanently crippled.

Today, years later, he is a gifted and much-loved worship leader at a church in a neighboring city. My reaction wounded him badly, and I wonder sometimes, *What if my lack of self-control had driven him out of ministry? What if I had derailed this good young man from doing what God designed him to do, and by extension, robbed those that he has fruitfully led from having the blessing of his influence in their lives?*

The other incident also involved a heavy word, but thankfully, it was a word delivered in grace. A young man in our church (whom I'll call Tom) began dating a woman who was separated from her husband. A divorce seemed imminent but had not yet occurred. She, of course, felt as if the marriage had been dead for a long time, and saw the divorce as nothing more than a legal formality. She was free to fall in love again, and she had.

I sat down with the dating couple. They were all smiles and all hands, practically on each other's laps, giddy with infatuation. "This isn't right," I told them, and their smiles were slowly replaced by tight lips and hard eyes. "She is a married woman," I told him, "with a husband hoping to reconcile. He is not your husband," I told her, "and you have no right to begin a romance with him, no matter how dead you believe your marriage to be."

To say the meeting got emotional would be an understatement. She sobbed and then shouted; he yelled, and then stood so he could yell louder. They stormed off in a torrent of profanity, slammed doors, and screeching tires, vowing never to return to this shitty, judgmental church. They didn't.

Nearly ten years later I was walking through an airport when I heard a familiar voice call my name. I turned to see Tom, hurrying to get up from the table where he was eating and make his way toward me. He grabbed my hand to shake it, then pulled me into a tight hug. "Man, I hated you so badly for confronting me back then. But I eventually heard you, and I got out of that relationship. I feel like you saved my life," he said, eyes wet and alive with feeling. "Would you like to meet my wife?" he asked with a shy smile, gesturing to a beautiful young woman still seated at the table. "We're on our honeymoon," he said, his face beaming.

As I reflect on the contrast between those two encounters, what immediately stands out to me is my ego. With the worship leader, I (wrongly) felt disrespected, and in my offended state I acted like a petty tyrant. I didn't ask him why he did what he did, and made no effort to understand what his actions meant to him. Instead, I imputed meaning to his actions, assumed his motives, and reacted accordingly. I used the power of my position to insist that he sit and listen while I scolded him, assigning motives to him that seemed right in my head but in fact were entirely inaccurate.

With Tom, thankfully, my ego wasn't part of the equation. I was able to speak an appropriately hard truth in a spirit of grace and love, and when things got heated, I didn't feel the need to defend or retaliate. And even though it was rejected at first, that word of truth spoken in the right spirit was eventually able to break through his defenses and bring freedom.

"A gentle tongue can break a bone," the Proverbs tells us (Prov 25:15). For the leader, our capacity to speak truth from a place of secure love and ego-free grace has everything to do with how we are allowing God to refine our ability to handle power.

BECOMING A PERSON WHO CAN BE TRUSTED WITH POWER

How does a leader, particularly a leader in a church plant where power could easily be abused, learn to use power well? What practices, attitudes, and postures can help us lean into Jesus' work in this area? Several come to mind that have proved fruitful for me and those I have been blessed to journey with.

Embrace the fact that you have power (and that this is a good thing). This may seem an obvious place to start, but it needs to be stated. For many leaders, when they are first awakened to the wreckage that can result from power improperly wielded, their reaction is to try to divest themselves of power—to make themselves powerless.

But sometimes in their caution, they swing the pendulum too far. Some do this by becoming ultrademocratic in their leadership style, deferential to the point that they are not leading so much as polling the group. While not as immediately destructive as the one who wields power recklessly, this is not a healthy alternative either. As we'll discuss in a later chapter, collaborative discernment and shared leadership are extremely important, and dispersing power into a team is itself an important check on a leader's power. But even in teams where this happens well, the planter still needs to understand the contours of their particular leadership role and style, and exercise it for the good of the church.

Do you feel God is giving you vision? Are there kingdom-shaped dreams on your heart? Do you have a nagging sense that something needs to be addressed, corrected, or advanced? Speak it! Put it out there, and invite the community of leaders to pray it, evaluate it, shape it, nuance it. The fact is, leadership is a gift God gives to some members of the body, and those who have this gift are commanded (commanded!) to lead with eager diligence (Rom 12:8). Embrace this, lean into it, and do it well.

Yes, pay attention to your instinct to lead with others, and discern with them God's will for the church. But don't abandon your role in the process. To abdicate this responsibility is to misuse one's gifts and ultimately to impoverish your congregation.

The root behind this error is a belief the cautious leader easily falls into: the trap of thinking that power is bad. Not so. Power used poorly is bad, but power put to good ends is good. In fact, good power is needed if the powers of darkness are to be beaten back by Christ's inbreaking kingdom! These words of Jesus are well known, so read them slowly:

> You know that those who are regarded as rulers of the Gentiles lord it over them, and their high officials exercise authority over them. Not so with you. Instead, whoever wants to become great among you must be your servant, and whoever wants to be first must be slave of all. For even the Son of Man did not come to be served, but to serve, and to give his life as a ransom for many. (Mk 10:42-45)

Note that in cautioning the disciples against misusing power, Jesus neither denies that they should have power, nor tells his disciples to divest themselves of it. Rather, he tells them that they are to *use their power for good*—to serve those under their charge, just as Jesus does.

We can mistakenly equate serving others with not having power, but the fact is that only those who have power are able to serve others. Jesus operated in tremendous power, and he imbues the disciples with his power, authorizing them to do the work of the kingdom:

When Jesus had called the Twelve together, *he gave them power and authority* to drive out all demons and to cure diseases, and he sent them out to proclaim the kingdom of God and to heal the sick. (Lk 9:1-2)

Jesus gives his disciples his power to do what he does (cf. Mt 4:23). The disciples find they really can use this power, and do so to good effect. When they return rejoicing, Jesus affirms what they have done in his power, while again cautioning the disciples to keep their power properly checked:

The seventy-two returned with joy and said, "Lord, even the demons submit to us in your name."

He replied, "I saw Satan fall like lightning from heaven. I have given you authority to trample on snakes and scorpions and to overcome all the power of the enemy; nothing will harm you. However, do not rejoice that the spirits submit to you, but rejoice that your names are written in heaven." (Lk 10:17-20)

Rather than trying to divest yourself of power or using it to enrich yourself, use it to benefit those around you.

"Yes, your power extends even over the evil spirits," Jesus seems to say, "but there are even bigger things to rejoice over than that."

Jesus reiterates this again in the Great Commission. "All the authority in the universe has been given to me," he says. The king is back. Therefore—*because of this authority*—we are *authorized* to go—to make disciples, to baptize, to teach people to live in his way.

Jesus has seen fit to give you power. Rather than trying to divest yourself of it or using it to enrich yourself, use it to benefit those around you.

Combine power with vulnerability. The self-aware leader will recognize that having power carries an element of danger. But if becoming powerless is not the right antidote, what is? And how do we prevent power from becoming a corrupting influence in our lives? Not by becoming powerless, but by becoming vulnerable.

Andy Crouch, in his penetrating book *Strong and Weak*, makes this observation: "We do not lack for authority. In Christ we have all the authority we need and more—'All things are yours' (1 Cor. 3:21). But what unlocks that authority is the *willingness to expose ourselves to meaningful loss*—to become vulnerable, woundable in the world."[3]

When we do this, Crouch argues, we are imitating Christ. "For this, too, is what it means to bear the divine image—if the One through whom all things are made spoke into being a world where he could be betrayed, wounded and killed. What we are missing, to become like him, is not ultimately more authority—*it is more vulnerability*."[4]

Part of what makes power intoxicating is its capacity to make us impervious to harm. The savvy leader quickly learns how to use power as a shield, preventing the embarrassment of our weaknesses being seen, protecting us from those who might criticize or tarnish our image, allowing us to avoid awkward questions by subtly side-stepping or shutting down those who would ask them.

We can all recall times when we didn't use power as a shield, and rather marched into ministry like the sons of Sceva—involuntarily vulnerable—fighting strong enemies and getting beaten silly (Acts 19:14-16). It is these experiences of being wounded, and the subsequent desire to avoid future wounds, that tell us we should hide behind our power. But this is the wrong solution. It is not vulnerability that we must avoid, but the temptation to *invulnerability*. Invulnerability is what makes us a danger to ourselves and those in our care.

To have power and voluntarily pursue vulnerability is counterintuitive, but it is in fact the way of Christ. It follows the pattern of the One who took on woundable flesh and blood, who stripped down to wash his disciples' feet, who ultimately chose a cross—not because he was forced to but because he wanted to (Jn 10:18). The choice to be vulnerable is the choice to love. This, and not self-protection, is the way of the servant leader.

I don't always do this well, but consciously modeling vulnerability for my church is one of my goals. Self-deprecation comes easy to me, which might help, but in my preaching and counseling I try to regularly tell stories about my weaknesses, struggles, and failures (1 Tim 4:15). When driving home harder truths, my admonishments and imperatives are stated as commands for us, not you. I'm convinced that whatever the Scriptures exhort the church to do applies doubly to me, and I try to speak the Word of God in a way that reflects this.

My biblical conviction is that while the pastoral role certainly is one of leadership, it is not meant to be an elevated position. Brennan Manning captured this for me meaningfully in his illustration of the church as a wagon train. In his allegory the pastor is neither the trail boss (the Father), the scout (Jesus), nor the buffalo hunter who provides the pioneers with meat (Holy Spirit). No, his job is far more modest. He is the cook who serves up whatever meat the buffalo hunter brings to feed the pioneers.[5] The pastor is not an exalted member of the community. He or she is simply another pioneer who has learned how to cook.

The pastor is merely one more member of the body who happens to have been gifted and given responsibility to lead, teach, and shepherd. We try to communicate this in a number of subtle ways. One of these is that my staff and I don't use titles. I introduce myself to new people as Tim, and invite the church to address me by first name. Only the church's kids (and a few adults who are more comfortable if they address me with a title) call me Pastor Tim. When we preach, we do so from the floor, not from a stage. We don't dress up but rather wear the same kind of clothes to church that everyone else does (which, in Southern California, means we are pretty casual). Practices like these are subtle, for sure, and I would bet most in our church have never given much thought to the reason we do them. Yet, as Martin Luther said, everything preaches. The understated way we conduct ourselves as pastors says something about how we view ourselves and, consequently, about our vulnerability.

Different churches and different cultures have different expectations of their clergy, so I realize the specific ways we approach this wouldn't work everywhere. But I think it's worth asking, What can I do in my context to demonstrate vulnerability? What would communicate that I as pastor am a fellow traveler, and not part of a vaunted class?

Find people you can submit to. Another way we add vulnerability to our power is by proactively seeking out accountability. Historically, this was known as the discipline of submission, and it was seen as essential to pastoral health and vitality.

In speaking to this need, Eugene Peterson invokes the old adage that "the doctor who has himself as a patient is a fool," which he then applies to pastors. "If those entrusted with the care of the body cannot be trusted to look after their own bodies, far less can those entrusted with the care of souls look after their own souls, which are even more complex than bodies and have a correspondingly greater capacity for self-deceit."[6]

We need someone to direct us more, not less, as we mature.

In the beginning, he says, pastors are self-motivated to be people of prayer, Scripture, and self-disciplined growth. But we need someone to direct us, because over time our passions cool and our disciplines slip. We need someone to direct us more, not less, as we mature. "On the lower slopes of the mountain, it never occurred to me to have a guide. But about halfway up the mountain, alarmed at how many maimed and dead bodies of other pastors I was seeing, I became frightened. Aware of the danger of the enterprise and my own ignorance of the mountain, I decided that I must have a skilled guide, a spiritual director."[7]

TOM EISENMAN, *SPIRITUAL DIRECTOR*

I do spiritual direction with Christian leaders. I have over fifty clients I meet with monthly, many of whom are church planters.

In first meetings with church planters, the stories I hear are often disturbingly similar. Most land somewhere on the overwhelmed scale, weighed down by crushing responsibilities, unrealistic expectations, and far too many squeaky wheels to grease.

Church planting is exhausting. Families of these pastors have to survive on time scraps, and marriages are frequently stretched to the breaking point. It's not uncommon for church planters to describe their reality using the familiar illustration of circus performers trying to keep dozens of plates all up and spinning on shaky poles. And more workshops on what to look for in poles and plates and how to improve spinning are not effectively alleviating the stress.

Pete Scazzero, a ministry crisis survivor, writes, "The overall health of any church or ministry depends primarily on the emotional and spiritual health of its leadership. In fact, the key to successful spiritual leadership has much more to do with the leader's internal life than with the leader's expertise, gifts, or experience."[8]

The apostle Paul knew this. A special wisdom is revealed in his earnest prayer that God would make you more "intelligent and discerning in knowing him personally, your eyes focused and clear, so that you can see exactly what it is he is calling you to do" (Eph 1:17-18 MSG). The secret isn't to double down on head knowledge; it is to learn to allow renewed knowledge to move through the head to your heart—knowledge transformed by the Spirit into heartfelt relationship—"knowing him personally." Paul also prays for the gift of spiritual eyes to discern God's present movement and emphasis. This is the called life. What is he calling me to do?

If we have been ensnared in a driven ministry agenda, powered by our natural selves, the result will always be fatigue, spiritual emptiness, stress, and burnout. The encouragement in Paul's prayer is to live and work out of a truly present-tense, personal relationship with Jesus. Fruitful, joyful ministry can become more of a daily reality when we identify our uniquely healthy rhythms and begin living each day from a more authentic center, our interior life of love.

I believe every church planter should have both a coach and a spiritual director. The coach knows church planting and can act more as a wise mentor, planner, and partner in problem solving. A spiritual director is trained to sit with you and listen compassionately to your story, noticing with you God moments and God's movements. They can help you find and maintain healthy rhythms of meaningful work and adequate rest and solitude. Only then can your exterior ministry enjoy health and vitality as it flows from a deep interior life in God.

Particularly in the early years of a church plant, accountability is sparse. We are still raising up leaders, and even structures like elders or a board are too young to meaningfully exert authority over us. It's up to us to proactively seek out—to invite—accountability. It won't come to us otherwise.

In the first few years of our church plant a key figure was Wayne, my church-planting coach. Wayne was not only a source of wisdom and practical advice but a careful student of my soul. "You are more important than what you do" was a frequent line I heard from him, and his questions reflected this. "How many hours are you working? What are you doing for rest and leisure? How would your wife say you are doing at being a husband these days?" And being wise enough to not just take my word for it, he would sometimes call my wife and ask her how I was doing as well!

A church planting coach is an invaluable asset. In fact, in the opinion of church-planting guru Bob Logan, "Getting a coach is the single most effective thing you can do as a church planter."[9] If your network or denomination does not provide you with one, I encourage you to seek one out. But more than that, don't just utilize your coach for ministry advice, *submit to them*. Invite them to speak into your life and ministry with ruthless honesty, and commit to taking their counsel with ruthless seriousness.

As the coaching phase ends, we will need to invite others into this role—our leadership teams or elders, a bishop or superintendent, a spiritual director, a trusted mentor, or a spiritually mature friend. But we must invite them—they will not come on their own.

These three—embracing power, seeking vulnerability, and inviting accountability—are not infallible, but they help us avoid the dangers of either rejecting power or misusing it.

When God created his good world, he made men and women in his image. Their role was not to be one of passive acquiescence, but one of power. We were made to rule under God as his governors, stewards of his authority as divine king.[10]

Exercising that power for the good of others is what we were made for.

We close this chapter with a final reminder from Martin Luther King Jr.:

> One of the great problems of history is that the concepts of love and power have usually been contrasted as opposites, polar opposites, so that love is identified with a resignation of power, and power with a denial of love. . . . What is needed is a realization that power without love is reckless and abusive and that love without power is sentimental and anemic. Power at its best is love, implementing the demands of justice, and justice at its best is love correcting everything that stands against.[11]

FOR REFLECTION AND DISCUSSION

1. What would it look like for you to properly embrace the power God has entrusted to you? Right now, are there areas where you wonder if you might be misusing that power?

2. What can you do in your context to demonstrate vulnerability? What would communicate that you as pastor are a fellow traveler and not part of a vaunted class?

3. Who are the people with whom you can be ruthlessly honest? Who are the people who love you enough to tell you the truth about yourself?

FURTHER RESOURCES

The Pastor by Eugene Peterson

Strong and Weak by Andy Crouch

The Way of the Dragon or the Way of the Lamb by Jamin Goggin and Kyle Strobel

5

OBSCURITY

Can I Minister Without Being Noticed?

*The question is not: how many people take you seriously?
How much are you going to accomplish? Can you show
some results? But: are you in love with Jesus?*

Henri Nouwen

I planted the seed, Apollos watered the plants, but God made you grow.

Paul the Apostle (1 Corinthians 3:6 MSG)

"Nearly all of my church planters feel like failures."
Dan served as the regional director of church planting for a large
denomination, and he was describing what had emerged as their
normal pattern. "We do our best to be discerning and only recruit
those that we think will be good planters. Despite that, 40 percent of
those churches never really take root, and they close in the first
couple years. Those planters, of course, are hurting deeply, and we
end up spending a lot of the energy we expected to put into the new
church into providing care for them and their families, and trying to
find other churches where they can serve."

I nodded sympathetically. I've heard this story many times
from a number of church-planting leaders in various networks
and denominations.

"But that's not the worst of it," he continued. "Of those that do make it, maybe 5 percent at most go on to be 'homerun hitters'—their ministry explodes, and within a few years they are pastoring a church of hundreds, or sometimes even a thousand or more. The rest go on to pastor normal-size churches—fifty, seventy-five, one hundred, maybe more. But they feel like failures because they aren't homerun hitters! The reality is, and what is so hard to help them see, is that they aren't failures—they are *normal pastors.*"

THE NEED TO BE EXTRAORDINARY

As a general rule, church planters are ambitious. For most, planting a church is a response to a need that burdens them to the point that they have to see it resolved—a holy discontent. When they look at their city, they see populations that aren't being reached by other churches, areas of injustice that are not being addressed, or missing gospel emphases that, if rediscovered, would lead to healthier, more robust followers of Jesus. The planter wants to start a church because their heart burns to bring the grace of Christ to bear upon those needs.

What happens if God chooses not to do big things through them but rather things that are, well, normal?

With that drive, there often comes a dose of grandiosity. Planters think big, dream even bigger, and at some level genuinely believe that God will do these big things through them.

But what happens if their reality doesn't match up to their dream? What happens if God chooses not to do big things through them (as they define big things) but rather things that are, well, *normal?*

Researcher Brené Brown describes our adverse reaction to this prospect as the "shame-based fear of being ordinary." She further describes this fear of normality as a sense of "never feeling extraordinary enough to be noticed, to be lovable, to belong, or to cultivate a sense of purpose."[1]

As planters, we have to ask ourselves, *Am I willing to plant, even if it means I may be nothing more than a normal pastor?* Or to state it a different way, *Am I willing to spend my life laboring for the glory of God, even if no one really notices?*

WHAT 90 PERCENT OF PASTORS HAVE IN COMMON

Increasingly, pastors are thinking about success in broader terms than the size of their church—a healthy trend for which we can all be grateful. But I want to begin this chapter by talking about church size, as it is one of the more tangible starting places for us as we consider this topic, and as it remains a source of either pride or insecurity for many planters.

Think with me about the implications of the following. According to Duke University's National Congregations Study (2012):[2]

- 43 percent of all US churches are fifty people or fewer
- 24 percent are between fifty and one hundred people
- 21 percent are between one hundred and 250 people
- 10 percent are between 250 and one thousand people
- 2 percent are one thousand people or more

Two additional stats from the Hartford Institute for Religion Research help round out the picture. First, the median size church in the United States is eighty (meaning half of all churches have more people, and half have less). Second, only half of 1 percent of churches are megachurches (two thousand or more congregants).[3]

What does this tell us?

It tells us that ordinarily, churches are small. The corollary: most pastors will lead small churches. Think about it this way: two-thirds of lead pastors will never shepherd a church of more than one hundred people; nine out of ten will never pastor more than 250; and only two pastors per thousand will lead a megachurch.

I came through seminary at a time when it seemed like every voice was shouting, "Your goal is to be a dynamic leader who will build a huge church!" This sentiment, even if usually more implicit than explicit, was so pervasive that I'm not sure I ever truly questioned it. Every author of every ministry book I read, every conference speaker, every article in *Leadership Journal*, was from a large-church pastor. "Successful pastors grow big churches," was the message. "Be like these people." What's more, the church where I was being mentored into ministry, and then the church I served right after seminary, were each churches of about three thousand! In my mind, what else could success entail but bursting through numerical barriers and pastoring a ginormous crowd of people?

But coming in contact with statistics like these made me rethink my assumptions. The fact of the matter is that the overwhelming majority—close to 90 percent—of churches are small (though the sheer mass of churches in that range suggests we might need to redefine what we mean by small). Even those that might be termed medium size are relatively few, and large churches, for all the attention they get, might best be considered an anomaly.

Though precise numbers are hard to come by, when we look at the global church, and also at the church historically, these numbers are only reinforced. Looking across cultures and throughout church history, we find that smaller churches have always been the norm. Larger churches happen, for sure, but they are outliers.

These facts lead me to one of two conclusions. Either 90 percent of all churches are failures—they didn't try hard enough, or didn't pray enough, or didn't employ the right methods to grow to a size that would deem them a success—or 90 percent of all churches are not failures, but are in fact as God intends them to be. Perhaps, rather than smaller size being a sign of something gone wrong, there is a reason that God most often chooses to arrange his people into family-size units, with large churches being more of the exception.

It didn't take me long to conclude that option B was more plausible. And this helped me rethink not just what constituted success,

Perhaps there is a reason that God most often chooses to arrange his people into family-size units, with large churches being more of the exception.

but how we as a new church might live out our mission as well.[4]

For instance, if God's normal pattern is to establish family-sized outposts of the kingdom throughout a given community, this gave us freedom to think differently about how we would reach people. We began to ask questions like, "What would it look like to plant ten churches of two hundred rather than one church of two thousand?"

Might that allow us to continue to grow and reach people, but also to foster a deeper connectedness that aids people in their discipleship to Jesus? And in doing so, might living as a family-sized church allow us greater capacity to know those we worship with each Sunday? To have the opportunity to know the names and stories of our fellow pilgrims? To know each other's children and help nurture them in the faith?

Is it possible that in smaller units, where it is harder to be anonymous and just assume someone else is taking responsibility for the church, that we might be able to foster greater ownership in God's mission? To avoid the football principle we so often witness—twenty-two people on the field working hard, and ten thousand in the stands watching them?

It freed us to consider that perhaps we didn't need to be everything to everyone, and instead ask, "Who are we?" And consequently, "Who might we best be positioned to reach in this city?" God would no doubt bring other congregations to reach those we weren't as good at reaching, and maybe even would do so through us, should we be fortunate enough to become a parent church.

As we considered global ministry, it prodded us to ask, "How might we, as a smaller church with limited resources, think creatively about how we might have the most impact? What would happen if, rather than taking a shotgun approach—doing global work wherever people's hearts were led—we took a laser-beam approach, prayerfully seeking God for one place in the world where we could make a twenty-year commitment?

This thinking led us to begin work in Mozambique, one of the poorest and least reached countries in Africa. For us at least, this approach has been beautifully fruitful. As of the time of this writing, that work has grown to include two orphanages, several microbusinesses where we teach people a trade, a pastoral training school, and nearly two hundred new church plants.[5]

MICRO, MEGA, AND EVERYTHING IN BETWEEN

Please don't mistake this as an anti–big-church rant. I rejoice in healthy missional churches that grow large every bit as much as healthy missional churches that are smaller, and I firmly believe that we need churches of every size—micro, mega, and everything in between—if we are to carry out the work of the King. Nor is this a head-in-the-sand view of how very difficult pastoring a small church can be. Every size church brings its own strengths and its own weaknesses, and we err to either romanticize or demonize churches of any particular size.

My point here is simply that as it comes to our work as church planters, it is important that we carry out our ministries with appropriate expectations. This isn't a minor consideration—a recent study found that appropriate expectations are one of four correlative factors in a church planter's success.[6]

When we buy into the lie that we are nothing more than a failed version of the celebrity pastor *du jour*, we have both misunderstood our calling and undermined our potential for kingdom impact.

The truth is, most pastors do minister—and always have—in obscurity, never being known outside the context of their immediate parish. And what is true of pastors in general will certainly be true for church planters as well. The norm will be obscurity.

"Well, I won't be one of the 'typical' pastors." Maybe not. But what if you are? Do you have the capacity to do the hard work of church planting even if it's in a smaller church? And perhaps more important, wouldn't you *like to be* the kind of pastor who can minister with joy whether you do so in obscurity or not?

"But I thought all healthy things grow." Yes, all healthy things grow, but we need to remember that all healthy things also have an optimal size. From oak trees to golden retrievers, we don't expect beautiful things to grow indefinitely. Once it reaches its optimal size, it grows in different ways, and if all goes well, it will produce entirely new growth through multiplication.[7]

The truth is, most pastors do minister—and always have— in obscurity.

It's easy to lose sight of that in an age of celebrity pastors where we perceive, contrary to the reality on the ground, that large churches are the norm. This is what Karl Vaters calls the "Grasshopper Myth"—not being small, but *feeling* small and believing those feelings.[8]

BECOMING A PASTOR WHO CAN MINISTER WITHOUT BEING NOTICED

I have always marveled at Jesus, who, upon seeing that the crowds are only following him for bread, issues a challenge to discipleship that intentionally drives people away. Potential disciples must not come solely for the food but must "eat the flesh of the Son of Man and drink his blood" (Jn 6:53). The crowd, many disciples included, dissipates.

And as if that isn't enough, Jesus then turns to the Twelve. He strikes me as almost surprised to see them. "Oh, are you still here?" he asks. "Do you want to leave too?" (Jn 6:67).

What a contrast to the insecurity out of which I typically minister. In the same situation, I picture myself in the parking lot calling out to departing cars, "Are you sure you want to go? Have you considered how well we do such and such?"

Yet Jesus is unruffled by the size of his following, be it large or small. Ten times in this passage he references the Father, and what the Father wills for him and those who would follow. "It isn't enough to come for the blessings I can give you," Jesus, in essence, says. "If you follow me, it needs to be because you want to ingest me—to get my life into yours in such a way that my life becomes yours, and my passion for the Father's will becomes yours."

I wonder if Jesus, looking at the shape of present pastoral ministry, isn't giving that same word to us as pastors. "You can't lead a church because you think I'll bless you with numbers, or reputation, or fame, or respect, or a platform. It has to be about who I am in you and in those you lead, and whatever things—big or small—the Father intends to do through you."

I feel like it took my first ten years as a planter to begin to understand this, and I still feel very much a novice at accepting my own relative obscurity. So how do we grow in our capacity to be pastors who can minister in obscurity? Not just grudgingly, but as ministers who can shepherd those who are in front of them with real joy, without worrying about those who are not? There are three practices that God is using to help me grow in this area.

Focus on building bigger Christians, not bigger churches. So just what exactly is it that I am supposed to be doing as a pastor? At times I'm surprised how difficult it can be to answer this question.

One of the texts that grounds me in my calling is found as an aside Paul makes in his plea to the church in Galatia:

> "My dear children, for whom I am again in the pains of childbirth until Christ is formed in you." (Gal 4:19)

Every part of this speaks to me.

"My dear children . . ." Re-read the opening verses of Galatians if you've forgotten how angry Paul is with this church. Yet he regards his wayward "children" with the tender affection of a loving parent.

"I am again in the pains of childbirth . . ." Suffering, repeatedly, is accepted as part of the pastoral call for Paul.

And especially, I'm grounded by what Paul identifies as the goal of his work: that *"Christ is formed in you."*

Here we have what, for me at least, is one of the Bible's most succinct and poignant job descriptions of the pastoral task: *helping our people be formed into the likeness of Jesus.*

I wonder how many of us, especially on this side of the church growth movement, have lost this as our primary goal? How many of us have abandoned this call in pursuit of making our churches—and by extension, ourselves—less obscure?

Perhaps no one has described this shift in modern pastoral identity as often and as compellingly as Eugene Peterson:

> The biblical fact is that there are no successful churches. There are, instead, communities of sinners, gathered before God week after week in towns and villages all over the world. The Holy Spirit gathers them and does his work in them. In these communities of sinners, one of the sinners is called pastor and given a designated responsibility in the community. The pastor's responsibility is to keep the community attentive to God. It is this responsibility that is being abandoned in spades.[9]

If we do indeed make growing bigger Christians our aim, will our church grow as well? It may. And I would argue that certainly your church's *impact* will grow, regardless of whether its numerical footprint does. But ultimately, I believe we do better to leave that to God. As Paul said, "I planted, Apollos watered, but God gave the growth" (1 Cor 3:6 ESV). Our job is to see people connect to Jesus in such a way that their inner life looks more like his inner life. God is the one who determines what church growth will or won't result.

Practice the discipline of secrecy. I recall with some pain one of Life Cov's first and most steadfast leaders. He was a terrific leader, about my same age, with gifts that complemented mine well. Where I was strong on vision and strategy, he was strong in administration and was great in seeing and implementing the steps needed to make our vision a reality.

But in spite of the fact that I loved him and had prayed for someone like him who was strong where I was weak, a part of me felt threatened. It was subtle, but I was slow to give him credit, to praise him privately or publicly for the great service he gave to our church. Irrational though it was, I somehow felt as if giving him credit diminished mine. I was frustrated with myself for being so petty. In my deepest heart I wanted to give praise away liberally, to those around me and to God, yet I struggled to live into this desire.

Jesus points us toward a remedy—a practice that has come to be known as the spiritual discipline of secrecy.

When we engage in spiritual practices, Jesus tells us, we have two options. If we are craving the praise and recognition of those around us, then, like the Pharisees, we can practice our disciplines in a way that calls attention to ourselves. Jesus gives three hyperbolic examples of this in Matthew 6: we can announce with trumpets when we give to the poor, pray loudly on busy street corners to attract attention, or get disheveled and put on a miserable face to let the world know we are fasting. When we choose this path, Jesus says, we may indeed be admired by others, but the pleasure of impressing those around us will be the totality of the benefit we receive.

The second option is to practice our disciplines subtly, for the sole purpose of pleasing our Father in heaven. When we give, we do so without bragging; when we pray, we do so in private, just us and God; when we fast, we wash up and put on a smile rather than wearing our misery on our sleeve. Then our offering to the Father will truly be an offering to the Father—not a thinly disguised attempt at elevating ourselves. When we engage in spiritual disciplines in this way, Jesus says, the benefits will be farther reaching and longer lasting: "Your Father, who sees what is done in secret, will reward you" (Mt 6:4, 6, 18).

Practicing the discipline of secrecy is as simple as this: do good things, and don't tell anybody.

In secrecy we let our actions be seen by the Father alone, and allow him alone to be the one to promote our actions. Or not, as the case might be. As Dallas Willard has put it, "Secrecy rightly practiced allows us to place our public relations department entirely in the hands of God. . . . We allow *him* to decide when our deeds will be known and our light will be noticed. . . . As we practice this discipline, we learn to love to be unknown and even to accept misunderstanding without the loss of our peace, joy, or purpose."[10] Handing this responsibility over to God, Willard concludes, is a tremendous *relief.*

Especially when I am feeling small in comparison to those I'm with, I find my PR department works overtime. When I am able to step back and truly listen to myself talk, it embarrasses me to see how adept I've become at self-promotion, the ease with which I've learned to work my spiritual resumé into conversation, the humble-brags I drop to show that I'm significant. These reveal the degree to which my identity is still wrapped up in my accomplishments, and not fully grounded in the deeper reality that I am God's beloved child.

The rewards Jesus references, the experience of the saints would indicate, includes multifaceted growth. The discipline of secrecy chastens and purifies our motives, slowly teaches us to be humble, to be ambitious for (rather than envious of) those around us, and to recognize and savor the quiet praise of the Father and of others as it comes. It helps us develop a heart that finds it natural to "Do nothing out of selfish ambition or vain conceit. Rather, in humility value others above yourselves" (Phil 2:3-4) and to declare with John the Baptizer, "He must become greater, I must become less" (Jn 3:30).

Embrace your own calling (and stop comparing yourself to others). In one of the most grace-filled moments in Scripture, the risen Jesus gives the recently washed-up Peter an opportunity to re-affirm his love. Three times—one for each of his three denials—Jesus invites Peter to confess, "Jesus, I love you."

"Feed my sheep," Jesus says in reply. Shake off your failure, dust yourself off, and get back in the game. But then Jesus says this: "When you are old you will stretch out your hands, and someone else will lead you where you do not want to go." Jesus said this to indicate the kind of death by which Peter would glorify God. Then he said to him, "Follow me!" (Jn 21:19).

Peter's attention turns to John, who was there too. "Lord, what about him?" Will John meet a similar end as Peter, dying for his faith?

"What is that to you?" Jesus replies. "You follow me."

Much of the angst that comes with obscurity is our focus on those who are not obscure. *Why them, and not me?* we wonder. Are they more worthy of that kind of fruit? Or just better than me? Is what I'm doing even worthwhile, paling as it does next to what is happening in their church?

I recognize the irony that the fact you are reading about obscurity in a book that I wrote makes me less obscure than most. But interestingly, getting published has been part of how God revealed to me just how much I was craving the praise of others, and how he has begun to heal me.

Two painful episodes drove this reality home for me. I remember vividly, just after the publication of my first book, eagerly looking forward to a book signing at my denomination's annual pastor conference. I was put at a book table with another author, a retiring seminary professor. He was a legend who had influenced our ministerium for decades. For an excruciating hour I stood next to him, forcing myself to smile, as a line of people patiently waited for an opportunity to shake his hand and get his signature. More than a few in line asked if I was his assistant. I believe in that hour I signed two books. I left feeling small, insignificant, and humiliated.

The second episode took place a few weeks later. I had been invited to lead a breakout session at a conference for young church leaders seeking innovative ways to engage a changing culture. This was the population I had written the book for, and I had dreamed of getting an invitation to this particular conference. But as it turns out, I was the smallest fish in a pond full of big fish. My book sat untouched at the far corner of the book table, my session barely attended, my presence inconsequential. I left feeling invisible.

The drive home was an angry one. "I needed this!" I fumed at God. "How will I ever get this book into the hands of those who need it if I don't get recognized?" In the storm that was my soul, I sensed God's voice gently saying, "Maybe what I gave you today was the thing you truly needed." I got quiet. And in that quiet, I came to recognize a truth I had been trying to ignore—that most of what I was craving was not for the book to help others but for it to help *me*. I craved recognition because I was insecure. I needed others to celebrate me so my fragile ego could be fed. I needed others to say I was valuable, because I had a hard time believing that if I heard it from God alone.

I was confronted that day with a question I deeply needed to hear. What if my calling—as a pastor, as a writer, as a teacher—is to continue to be a small fish in the pond? Will I be content—scratch that, *joyful*—in that call? Friend, what if that is your calling too? Will you still receive it? Will you still labor if only God and a handful of others ever take notice?

I appreciate my friend Kevin Haah's wise words here: "The definition of success is not what happens, not the result—that is God's issue. Instead, the definition of success is figuring out what God wants us to do and doing it."[11]

One more writing story. I knew God was growing me in this area when a few years ago I was invited to do a weekend conference for a great church. The first night I was walking through the lobby, flanked by posters featuring my likeness or pictures of my book cover that had been used to advertise the event. Attendees walked past, smiling or shyly looking away as they recognized me as the speaker. I made my way past some kind well-wishers to the restroom, and doubled over in laughter once I got inside. There, I found one more poster—this one posted directly above a urinal. I snapped a picture and sent it to my wife, who also laughed until she cried. I still have the picture, and it reminds me to keep any accomplishments in proper perspective.

I want to conclude this chapter with a prayer that has become important to me. It is commonly known as John Wesley's Covenant Prayer, and it helps me get centered when I find myself making ministry too much about me:

> I am no longer my own, but yours.
> Put me to what you will, rank me with whom you will;
> put me to doing, put me to suffering;
> let me be employed for you, or laid aside for you,
> exalted for you, or brought low for you;
> let me be full,
> let me be empty,
> let me have all things,
> let me have nothing:
> I freely and wholeheartedly yield all things
> to your pleasure and disposal.
> And now, glorious and blessed God,
> Father, Son and Holy Spirit,
> you are mine and I am yours. So be it.
> And the covenant now made on earth, let it be ratified in heaven.
> Amen.

Lord, make it so.

MICHAEL CARRION, *SENIOR PASTOR AND GENERAL OVERSEER OF THE PROMISED LAND COVENANT CHURCHES, BRONX, NEW YORK*

I was working on my third-ever sermon for Promised Land Church when I first heard Dr. Noel Jones's choir sing "It's Not About Us." I was a new seminary student and a new church planter, and was so very excited to share the gospel with our small South Bronx missional community.

I needed a study break, so I put on YouTube and clicked on his video. I remember being totally mesmerized at how big the choir was, how in sync they were as they sang praises to the king of glory, and the very tangible energy that seemed to jump from the video into my headphones.

As the music carried me to a place of reflection, I began to wonder, *Will we ever sound that good? Will our choir ever be that size? For that matter, will our congregation ever be the size of that choir?* I mean, that was a huge choir! It was bigger than most of the churches I had attended, and they probably wouldn't even fit into the small chapel where our church gathered.

Soon I began to feel incredibly discouraged and insanely inadequate. Did I have the right stuff to fulfill the call and handle the task of leading others to Jesus in one of the most economically disenfranchised communities in America? Before long I was systematically creating a mental list of why I was a failure—all while I had barely begun the work of building a core team! *Who did I think I was, trying to engage in such a feat?* I was a no-name charismatic preacher from an obscure Afro-Caribbean council of churches known more for their legalistic leanings than for planting healthy missional churches. I mean, no one had ever heard of me, and anyone who had heard of me knew there wasn't much to remember! (Can you tell I needed serious spiritual direction?)

I went into prayer—real prayer, wailing prayer. As I surrendered my heart to God's will, the Lord spoke to me as clearly as I have ever heard: "You don't need your name. You need *my* name. You didn't call yourself. This is *not* about you or your core team—this is all about how they see you surrender to me, and you speaking life, truth, grace, and the redemption found only at the cross." He went on. "Your list of shortcomings is really just passive complaints about being out of control. Trust me. Say what I tell you to say, when I tell you to say it. All of your brokenness, pain, and anxiety are going to be used to grow you up and strengthen you as I work through you."

That was seven churches, three charter schools, and three national social justice movements ago. And still, I am learning to make it about him and not me. I make it a practice to sit in the back row of the church. Most newcomers think I am one of the ushers, audio visual support, or a security guard. The same is true in our charter school network. I walk the halls somewhat awkwardly, like a new teacher who is lost and trying to find his assigned classroom. Most of our teachers don't even know I am the founder of the school.

Missio Dei for my life is not about introducing people to me, but to the goodness of Jesus Christ. May his name be ever lifted, and may he receive all of the glory for all that is done for the expansion of his kingdom through a nameless, unknown man like me.

FOR REFLECTION AND DISCUSSION

1. Do you relate to Brené Brown's "shame-based fear of being ordinary"? What kind of defense mechanisms do you see yourself erecting to prevent others from seeing you as ordinary?

2. The author summarizes pastoral ministry as "helping our people be formed into the likeness of Jesus." What would you add to or

take away from this description? How does your description differ if you are in a large or a small church?

3. What practical steps could you take when you find you are comparing yourself to other pastors or churches?

FURTHER RESOURCES

Life Without Lack by Dallas Willard

In the Name of Jesus by Henri Nouwen

The Strategically Small Church by Brandon J. O'Brien

The Grasshopper Myth by Karl Vaters

6

FAILURE

Am I Resilient in the Face of Setbacks and Defeats?

Courage is not simply one of the virtues, but the form of every virtue at its testing point.

C. S. LEWIS

When they saw the courage of Peter and John and realized that they were unschooled, ordinary men, they were astonished and they took note that these men had been with Jesus.

LUKE THE PHYSICIAN (ACTS 4:13)

"WHY THE HELL DID YOU DO THAT?"

When I was in high school, I decided I needed to play sports. I had dabbled in sports in my preteen years because my dad wanted me to learn the lessons that team sports have to teach. But I was terrible. Growing up, I never had the least bit of athletic ability. I was small and uncoordinated, and my body could be charitably characterized as having an utter lack of muscle. What's more, I just wasn't that interested. (Except in dodgeball, where I was a virtual ninja. Games that required one to avoid contact with the ball seemed to be my forte.) I was "the smart kid," never to be confused with any of the athletic kids.

When high school came, I wanted to give organized sports another try, in part to feel a part of a team and in part to try to up my chances in dating. I was too small to play football and lacked the skills to play basketball or baseball, so I opted for volleyball. To my surprise, from day one I loved the game, and after four long years had mustered just enough skill that my face didn't flush red with embarrassment as soon as I stepped onto the court.

But in my first year, I had what turned out to be a defining moment, though it took me a number of years to fully understand its significance. We were in the final high-pressure minutes of a close game, and much to my surprise the coach decided to put me in. Our team served the ball, and the other team executed a perfect bump, set, and spike back to our side of the net. The ball was moving at Mach speed directly toward me. No one else was in a position where they had any chance of getting to it—this was clearly my play.

Instinctively I dove hard for the ball, body fully extended, my right arm stretched out in front of me. The ball was traveling fast, but I was there first. My hand arrived at the spot the ball was headed a split second before the ball did. But at the last possible instant, a nanosecond before receiving the ball, I pulled my hand back. The ball hit the floor, the ref's whistle blew, and my coach hit the roof. Our entire bench was on their feet shouting in dismay, as were the fans in the stand. I was pulled out of the game as quickly as I went in, and the coach was right in my face, demanding, "Why the hell did you do that? Why did you let that ball go?"

"I . . . I don't know," I stammered. And I really didn't. Why, when I would want nothing more than to make a dramatic, game-changing play—to be the hero, to impress my team and the crowd—would I pull back my hand? I was desperate to be seen as something other than the brainy kid who excelled at school and little else. Why did I pull back?

The answer I eventually came to was painful to admit, but the pattern it revealed in my life was unmistakably true. I could endure failure, but only if I gave less than my best effort.

I discovered that my inner script went something like this: if I attempted something but didn't give it all I had, then if I failed, some part of me could still say, "Well, if I had tried harder I might have been able to pull it off." My failure wasn't absolute because I might have produced a different outcome had I tried harder.

But, if I gave 100 percent effort and *still* failed, what did that say about me? In that case I had nowhere to hide. I had no choice but to admit I had failed. And perhaps, worse yet, that *I was a failure*.

Without knowing it, that day I exposed a subtle defense mechanism that I had developed in which I would only give all of myself to endeavors at which I was certain I would succeed. In everything else, I might give some effort, but not all. In the years since, this incident became a bit of a parable for me—a physical demonstration of what I would do in other areas of life, including my leadership as a pastor. When I get scared, I pull back.

WHY WE TINKER WHEN WE SHOULD BE LEADING

It had been a season of fruitful growth, so Erwin McManus thought the church elders wanted to meet to congratulate him on a job well done. Instead, they gently expressed disappointment. "You aren't leading at full strength," they said. "We feel like something is holding you back." Devastated, McManus shared the incident with his wife, hoping to be comforted. Instead, she confirmed their opinion.

McManus was so angry he stopped the car in the middle of the road. He writes, "I sat there defending myself, all the while knowing the painful truth: I was afraid. I was hesitant. I was apprehensive and uncertain. It wasn't that I didn't know what to do; it was that I understood the consequences. Leadership comes with a price. I thought I could hide behind a measure of success and never be found out. I was not leading; I was tinkering."[1]

In my years as a pastor, I've awakened dozens of times to that same realization. I know what to do, but I'm afraid to do it. I don't want to risk failure, so I pull back. I tinker when I should be leading.

Why is this? Why is the fear of failure so debilitating? Why do we tend to shrink back rather than lead with courage? Two primary reasons come to mind.

First, I shrink back because I'm afraid of losing my gains. Anytime we fight hard to gain ground, advance an agenda, or make progress on something we care about, the thought of losing what we've worked for is scary. To do something new, to innovate, to start off in a new direction—while the adventure of it may be enticing, the potential loss looms in our mind. What if it doesn't work? What if people lose confidence in me or decide I'm no longer worth following?

This is especially true in those early days of a church plant when everything feels so fragile. Every new person who joins feels like a victory, and when anyone leaves, it feels like defeat.

This is also true in another way of a church as it matures, as the weight of decisions made now effects a larger group of people. If this doesn't work, what impact will it have on our present ministries and commitments? Will we still be able to pay the staff whose families are trusting me for a paycheck? To fund our orphans and missionary staff an ocean away? To pay the rent and keep the lights on where our worshipers gather each Sunday?

We have stood at such crossroads many times as a church, and they have always been difficult. Two of the most difficult times for me have involved theological stances that I knew would be unpopular with a significant chunk of the congregation.

In one instance, I was becoming aware of an area where we were not living into the Bible's teaching nearly as well as we needed to. To be faithful to the God of the Scriptures would require us to adjust our thinking and our practice in ways that were going to rock the boat, big time.

The second instance did not involve a change on our part but rather reiterating and clarifying a view we had always held, but which had recently become unpopular. The culture had shifted, and with it, a number of our congregants felt a temptation to shift too. To reiterate and clarify the Bible's teaching was going to come at a cost. Just how big a cost was unknown, and I was worried.

Both of these instances would involve a long season of patient teaching, gently instructing those who were opposed (à la 2 Tim 2:25), and wise, incremental changes in how the church functioned. Both would alienate a number of congregants, including ones I dearly loved, and several influential leaders. Both shifts would mean an unknown number of people getting angry, and some leaving the church. Hard-fought gains would be endangered, and ground would be lost.

But in both of these instances, I knew it came down to one baseline, rock-bottom question: *Will I lead us to be obedient to the Bible's teachings, even though it will be costly? Or will I shrink back?*

The second reason we shrink back, for many of us, cuts even deeper—the fear of losing face.

If one peruses secular leadership writing, you primarily find technique-based approaches to leading change. Noted business professor Robert Quinn surprised his readers by reframing leadership in terms that had more to do with the soul—identifying the primary obstacle leaders face not as external, but internal. Leading change, he writes, means "walking naked into the land of uncertainty."[2]

To lead change is not just to risk the loss of organizational gains, daunting as that is. No, leading change is also to risk the loss of self. If we try and we fail, our reputation, our standing, and the respect we want to see in the eyes of colleagues and congregants are all called into question. For many, this prospect is even more crippling than the potential loss of gains.

I would love to say that I am secure in this aspect of leadership, but I am not. I confess this is one of my perpetual struggles. How will others see me? How will this decision, and the potential losses it may incur, effect the ways my church sees me? My pastoral peers? The denominational leaders whose respect I desire? My wife, my kids, my parents?

This is where the hardest work comes—in overcoming my own sense of shame when I fail. Can I as a pastor find sufficient security in Christ, and who I am in him, that I am willing to absorb hits to my appearance before others?

Can I find sufficient security in Christ, and who I am in him, that I am willing to absorb hits to my appearance before others?

The reality, as some deep part of us already knows, is that it is in resisting the fears that we find the path to freedom. Succumbing to fear and pulling back only leads to more bondage. Leading despite the fears is a painful path, yes, but ultimately, if we persist in it, we find freedom. Freedom from being beholden to the views and judgments of others, freedom to faithfully lead as God directs, freedom to operate for his approval alone.

Dan Allender says a leader is beginning to realize this freedom when they become "disillusioned," by which he means they have accepted and worked through the grief that follows failure. He writes,

Clearly the disillusioned and best leaders are those who have nothing left to prove because they have known both failure and success. Failure teaches us to not fear the contempt of others. Success teaches us to not trust the applause of others. When contempt and applause no longer move your heart to hide or to strive then you are ready to ask the question, "What will please you, God?"[3]

LEARNING TO LEAD WITH COURAGE

How do we get there? How do we become men and women who can overcome our tendency to pull back, and instead act boldly in the face of failure? Who don't just tinker, but rather lead with courage? Three practices come to mind.

Recalibrate what you mean by failure. The psalmist asks, "Lord, who may dwell in your sacred tent? Who may live on your holy mountain?" His answer includes this arresting line: it is the one "who keeps their oath, even when it hurts" (Ps 15:1, 4).

My reflex is to define failure as people thinking ill of me, or people leaving the church, or us having to make painful budget cuts because the unpopularity of a decision has wreaked havoc on our finances. But a deeper part of me knows that definition is exactly backward.

When I really let myself think about it, there is another kind of failure, a deeper failure, that I fear more. That's the failure to do what I know is right because I'm afraid of the pain that may result. I want to be a leader, like the psalmist describes, who does the right thing even when it hurts.

There is a passage in one of Eugene Peterson's books that I've read dozens of times, particularly when I feel myself getting wobbly in the face of an unpopular decision. In it, he channels what he imagines a congregation would tell us when they call us to lead them, if only they had the awareness and the words to give voice to these unspoken desires. They know at some level, Peterson contends, that they need our help keeping and living their beliefs when storms hit and life gets confusing. The imaginary congregants say:

> We need help in keeping our beliefs sharp and accurate and intact. We don't trust ourselves; our emotions seduce us into infidelities. We know we are launched on a difficult and dangerous act of faith, and there are strong influences intent on diluting or destroying it. We want you to give us help. Be our pastor, a minister of Word and sacrament in the middle of this world's life. Minister with Word and sacrament in all the different parts and stages of our lives—in our work and play, with our children and our parents, at birth and death, in our celebrations and sorrows, on those days when morning breaks over us in a wash of sunshine, and those other days that are all drizzle. This isn't the only task in the life of faith, but it is your task. We

will find someone else to do the other important and essential tasks. This is *yours:* Word and sacrament.

One more thing: We are going to ordain you to this ministry, and we want your vow that you will stick to it. This is not a temporary job assignment but a way of life that we need lived out in our community. We know you are launched on the same difficult belief venture in the same dangerous world as we are. We know your emotions are as fickle as ours, and your mind is as tricky as ours. That is why we are going to *ordain* you and why we are going to exact a *vow* from you. We know there will be days and months, maybe even years, when we won't feel like believing anything and won't want to hear it from you. And we know there will be days and weeks and maybe even years when you won't feel like saying it. It doesn't matter. Do it. You are ordained to this ministry, vowed to it.

There may be times when we come to you as a committee or delegation and demand that you tell us something else than what we are telling you now. Promise right now that you won't give in to what we demand of you. You are not the minister of our changing desires, or our time-conditioned understanding of our needs, or our secularized hopes for something better. With these vows of ordination we are lashing you fast to the mast of Word and sacrament so you will be unable to respond to the siren voices.[4]

Yes, this is my role. The truth is, I took a vow by which I am "lashed to the mast"—bound to faithfully administer Word and sacrament, whether that makes people happy or not, in stormy weather or fair, whether the ship looks as if it will make it or crash on the rocks.

I am to speak God's Word, not just when it teaches and comforts, but when it rebukes and corrects (2 Tim 3:16). I will be wise, I will be gentle, and I will walk with those who struggle, but if I am to be faithful to the task given to me, I *will* speak even the hard truths, I *will* lead us even on paths that are hard. To do less—*that* is failure, and of a much more significant sort than the kind we can count in nickels and noses.

I was reminded of this last week when I was preparing a message for our church. The text pointed to a hard truth I needed to speak, and I could feel my reticence—my propensity to pull back. Then, during my devotions I read these words: The church's leaders "must hold firmly to the trustworthy message as it has been taught, so that they can encourage others by sound doctrine *and* refute those who oppose it" (Titus 1:9).

What does success mean in this instance? It is trusting that God's Word is worthy of trust, so much so that I am not afraid to speak it. Gracefully, yes, and with patience for those who struggle to accept it. But I must speak, whether people are encouraged or refuted. That morning I wrote in my journal, "I need to let go of the belief that the church will fail if people leave. It's true, if enough leave the church will close. But that's not failure. If we compromise our values or tolerate sinful behavior to get people to stay, and by doing so allow an unhealthy culture to dominate, *that* would be failure."

A little further in the passage Paul reminds us of the goal: "Our great God and savior, Jesus Christ . . . gave himself for us to redeem us from all wickedness and to *purify for himself a people* that are his very own" (Titus 2:13-14).

Not just people, but people *purified.*

My job is not to make people happy, but to make them holy. To pull back from doing so because I fear the cost—that would be failure.

Love God above your ambitions. Closely related to our definition of failure, we need to be honest about the nature of our love for God and our love of success.

Phil Vischer, the creative genius who founded VeggieTales, saw his company grow from a modest startup to a worldwide phenomenon with an annual revenue of over $40 million. But his life's work imploded when a lawsuit forced the company into bankruptcy. Phil was undone. "Fourteen years of work flashed before my eyes—the characters, the songs, the impact, the letters from kids all over the world. It all flashed before my eyes, then it all vanished."[5]

Sitting in the aftermath, Phil was forced to grapple with how much of his identity was wrapped up in his accomplishments. It was in this season of grief that he heard a pastor suggest that if God gives you a dream, then shows up in a way that makes that dream a reality, and then that dream *dies*, God may be testing you to see what you find more important—him or the dream.

All at once Phil was struck with the realization that much of his love for God had actually been love for his *dream*—for the ministry and impact he might have for God, not love for God himself. Painful though the season was, it was pivotal for Phil's growth. He writes, "At long last, after a lifetime of striving, God was enough. Not God and impact, not God and ministry, just God."[6]

It is easy as church planters, ever teetering on the brink of failure, to be consumed with our church succeeding, whether we define that as achieving a certain level of thriving or merely as surviving. To see our church grow to be fruitful is a holy longing. Yet, like any other good thing, if we begin to love that thing more than we love God, it has become an idol. And this particular idol has the side effect of fueling our fear of failure.

Every church planter needs the regular gut check of honestly evaluating his or her loves. What do I love more: God, or what God does for me? The approval of the Father, or the applause of those who deem me successful? The quiet attestation of the Spirit that we are doing the right thing, or the rush of seeing ministry impact? To be sufficiently free from fear and courageous to really lead, we need to come to a place where Jesus is enough.

Fail loudly. Shame and insecurity being what they are, most of us respond to failure by hiding. We reach for our proverbial fig leaf (i.e., an area of unquestioned strength) and try to hide behind it in order to mitigate our feeling of being exposed as weak. But the truth is that those leaders who are willing to be public about their failures actually do the most good for themselves and those they lead.

Andy Crouch tells about a study that followed a cohort of middle managers over the course of their careers, to see why some advanced into senior leadership and some did not. When the study concluded, there was only one factor that set apart the more successful managers: the speed and degree to which they owned their failures. When something went wrong in their area of responsibility, one group acted as if everything was fine when it wasn't, and did their best to keep their bosses and peers from seeing where they were lacking. This strategy proved ineffective in the long run, as this group experienced less career advancement. But, contrary to what many would expect, those who were most public with their failings advanced further in their careers over time. Crouch concludes, "The ones who succeeded were the ones who failed loudly, quickly, and boldly—rather than softly, timidly, and slowly."[7]

I struggle with this. I'm too proud and have too much of my ego wrapped up in my accomplishments. When I fail, I'm embarrassed, and the last thing I want is to look incompetent in front of others. But the counterintuitive truth is that if I want to lead well, my incompetence is exactly what I need to let others see. "Church planting," it seems, "is kryptonite for pride."[8]

Practically speaking, what does this look like? Own your mistakes. Apologize without delay, privately and publicly. And don't underestimate the importance of laughing at yourself.

After a lifetime of seminary teaching, one of my professors, Dr. Eddie Gibbs, had boiled down his most important pieces of advice for pastors to a handful of pithy maxims. The one I found most surprising was, "Don't take yourself too seriously." Huh? *This* is one of the most important things a pastor can do for their church?

But as I thought it about it more, I could see the wisdom. Think about it: what better way to model grace than to give it to yourself? To let your people watch you attempt hard things, and when you fail, to see you dust yourself off and try again? If you want to create a church culture where people feel empowered to attempt innovative

The church that wants to innovate must celebrate effort, not success. And this also means celebrating failure.

ways of being the church, they need to not only see what praise awaits them if they succeed, but what it will look like in those inevitable times when they fail. The truth is, you and I as pastors set the tone. If we take ourselves so seriously that we can't laugh at our failings, no one else will dare laugh at their own either.

An important corollary here is that the church that wants to innovate must celebrate effort, not success. And this also means celebrating failure.

One such critical moment occurred in our church's first year. One of our ministry team leaders had organized an outreach event for a subset of our community. This was one of our first attempts at outreach, and people's hopes were high. His idea was good, the plan was sound, and the team executed well. But it flopped. Nobody came—not one person. So how, I wondered, should I handle this? Part of me wanted to say nothing, so as not to further embarrass this leader. But what would my silence communicate to the church? Would others think I was embarrassed of or disappointed in him? That I had lost confidence in his leadership?

What I ended up doing (with this leader's permission) was to let it be a loud fail. The following Sunday when I stood up to teach, I went on and on about how great the idea was, how hard the team worked to put it together, the attention to detail, and even the financial expense. And then, with a smile and a shrug, I said, "And you know what? It was a bust—no one came." The room responded with a nervous chuckle, not sure how they should react. Then I added, "But you know what? I am so proud to be part of a church where people are willing to dream big, work hard, and take chances to reach our community. Not every idea—even every good idea—is going to work out. But I am sure grateful to be part of a church that is willing to go for it!" Then I brought the leader up front and presented him with a thank you card and a small gift, while the congregation cheered and hollered their approval.

JILL RILEY, *THREE-TIME CHURCH PLANTER, WASHINGTON AND MONTANA*

We knew this church plant would be a risky one. What we didn't know was just how much it would wear us down, nor did we anticipate that a day would come when we would have to shut its doors for good.

My desire was to plant in a location where the "haves" and the "have-nots" would circulate with one another with relative social ease. This placed us in a part of town that was between the theater/dinner district and the homeless shelters. It was also a place where no other churches existed.

By doing this we intentionally engaged a community of people who were steeped in poverty, addiction, mental illness, family trauma, recidivism, and troubles with the law. While we were resolute to minister to and with the community at our front doors, for me, the price it came with was living with chronic, low-grade fear.

One gentleman who frequented my office was a drug-addicted, unpredictable, violent offender. A woman with borderline personality disorder would threaten ruin upon me or the church if I made her unhappy. A man abused his wife until she tried to commit suicide, and then he denied her medical attention. Another would call me on Sunday mornings from the local jail just to let me know he would not be able to make it to church because he had been incarcerated again.

My office was located near the men's shelter, and those who had been rejected from the shelter because they were not sober or were sexual offenders would gather and talk outside my window. Within my earshot the men would stand and talk about me in sexual and violent fantasy innuendos.

Engaging the highly needy was already a daunting task because of all the services and support needed to minister to this population. However, the personal battle for me was my growing fear. I feared for my own safety, and for the future of my family should something happen to me.

But I soldiered on. With prayer, advice from those who were more experienced, and determination to minister to those God brought me, we continued to throw ourselves into the work. This "faith before fear" attitude helped me succeed in the short term as we were able to bring God's love to a group that desperately needed it. But long term was a different story.

Where I feel I ultimately failed was in maintaining balance. Within our congregation, we simply did not have a sufficient number of people who were spiritually and emotionally strong enough to help buoy our work. And it turns out that I needed more support than I thought I would if I was going to adequately serve this marginalized population. Witnessing the fallout from murder, abuse, kidnapping, knife fights, and more took its toll. Eventually, I became overwhelmed and stressed, to the point of my mental health fracturing.

Looking back, if I had the opportunity to do things differently, I would still engage the people of that underserved community, because that is what God had called me to do. What I would have done differently, however, is to wait to plant our church until my own spiritual and emotional foundation were healthy enough to hold the inevitable burdens that come with this sort of call. A better foundation would have helped us to minister with greater longevity. As it was, I didn't have the reserves to call on when extra effort was needed, and my mental decline caused the church to close, leaving a hole in our community and a deep sadness in my heart.

This incident could have easily slipped by and probably would have been quickly forgotten. But looking back, I'm convinced that was actually a pivotal moment for us in setting a tone for proactive and innovative ministry for years to come.

How ironic that one of the reasons we pull back is fear of losing our gains, while in reality it is in risking—and occasionally failing— that we create the sort of environment where people feel empowered to pursue innovation. And it's also ironic that we pull back to avoid losing face, when owning weakness actually serves to endear us to those around us.

I want to conclude this chapter with one of my favorite Scriptures on courage. In the first healing miracle after Jesus' resurrection, Peter and John found themselves on trial before the same Jewish leaders who had crucified Jesus. Asked to explain their actions, the disciples responded with a bold, unflinching confession of faith.

Then Luke gives us this line: "When they saw the courage of Peter and John and realized that they were unschooled, ordinary men, they were astonished, and they took note that *these men had been with Jesus*" (Acts 4:13).

Oh, that this would be said of me. What is courage? We could say courage is fear that has been with Jesus. As with every area of spiritual competency—and really, every good thing we need to lead a new church—all roads lead back to abiding in him.

FOR REFLECTION AND DISCUSSION

1. Can you identify one hard conversation you need to have but have been avoiding? Will you commit to having that conversation this week?

2. Similarly, can you identify any changes or adjustments you need to make but have been avoiding? What steps can you take toward making these a reality?

3. Do you need to surrender a potential loss or outcome in order to make a needed change?

4. As you commit to action in these areas, make this your prayer:

O eternal God, who has made all things for man, and man for your glory, sanctify my body and soul, my thoughts and my intentions, my words and my actions, that whatever I think, speak, or do may bring glory to your name, and by your blessing be effective and successful. Let no pride or self-seeking, no covetousness or revenge, no impure motives, no small thinking or small dreaming pollute my spirit and make my words or actions unholy. Let my body be a servant of my spirit, and both body and spirit servants of Jesus. (Jeremy Taylor, "A Prayer for Holy Intention in the Pursuit of Any Considerable Action")

FURTHER RESOURCES

Fail by J. R. Briggs

An Unstoppable Force by Erwin McManus

Renovation of the Church by Kent Carlson and Mike Lueken

7

PACE

Am I Treating Church Planting like
a Marathon or like a Sprint?

The main obstacle to love for God is service for God.

Henri Nouwen

I came that they may have life, and have it abundantly.

Jesus (John 10:10)

"There are two ways that a pastor can lead: as a motor-boat captain, or as a sailboat captain."

The group was a collection of pastors from the cluster of cities that make up that part of Los Angeles known as the South Bay. Once a month we gather for coffee, fellowship, and prayer, and occasionally to collaborate on a ministry venture or to be equipped by an outside speaker. In reality I think the main reason we keep coming back is that it's nice to walk into a room where, before you even open your mouth, everyone else understands what your life is like.

This was our first regular meeting since moral failure had ended the ministry of the pastor who had founded and led the group for the past decade.

I had invited our speaker, Kurt Fredrickson, because he knows something about what lends itself to healthy and unhealthy ministry. After over twenty years as a pastor, he was now an associate dean at Fuller Seminary, working with seasoned pastors as they pursued their Doctor of Ministry degrees.

"As a younger pastor," Kurt said, "I led like the captain of a motorboat. Because it was my hand on the rudder, I was in control. I knew where the church needed to go, and I was taking the boat full throttle in that direction. Swimmers and ducks beware if they got in the way!"

Many in the room chuckled and nodded. It was a style of leadership we were well acquainted with.

"But over time I began to suspect this might not be the best way to lead. I was exhausted, and as I looked around at our church, they were too. And if I slowed down long enough to be honest with myself, I couldn't deny that a lot of people were getting run over or buried in my wake. Eventually I admitted I had to learn a better way to lead—one that would be healthy and sustainable for me and for the church.

"Over time I recognized that Jesus was teaching me to lead in a different way—more like a sailboat captain. Sail boaters don't just point the boat in the direction they want to go and hit the gas—they pay attention to currents, wind, and waves. Sometimes the ride is fast and exhilarating, but at other times it is slow and restful. Sailboat captains can't just be about their hand alone on the rudder. For best results, they need to allow for others' hands to work the lines and trim the sails. In short, sailboat captains have to lead from a place of sensitivity, discernment, and community—not a place of control." Kurt paused. "It took me a long time to learn a different pace of ministry, mostly because it meant taming my ego's need to show myself 'successful.' But I think it probably saved my ministry."[1]

The room was silent, almost somber. I could see on people's faces that they were reflecting, some maybe about our friend whose ministry had just ended, and all of us about our own ministries. Unspoken questions lingered in the air: *What drives me to lead the way I do? Am I able to give up the control that comes with being a motorboat captain? Would I even be capable of leading more like a sail boater?*

CHOOSING A FLOURISHING LIFE

I've been the pastor of a church plant for sixteen years, and I can count on my fingers the number of days I have checked everything off of my to-do list.

The work is endless. There is always one more person to call, another hour of prep that would make that message stronger, another email to send, something else I need to learn. If we don't set up boundaries around how much we work, we will be consumed.

In chapter two I made the assertion that, contrary to how most church planters are wired, church planting needs to be treated like a marathon, not a sprint. Like a runner, we have to match our pace to the distance we want to travel. And like a sailboat captain, we have to work with currents and winds, invite others to participate in the work, and allow for variances in intensity from one season to the next for the sake of our health and those around us.

There have been seasons when, looking at the church planters I'm working with, I've felt like a majority are in danger of burnout. That's why I wanted to circle back and give a whole chapter to this topic. I believe learning to live at a healthy pace is at the heart of the spiritual competencies we need to develop if we are going to flourish as planters.

As planters, we have to make a *choice* to live in a way that will bring the abundant life of Jesus to our souls, our churches, and our families. No one else will do this for us.

But even as I write the word *choice* I hesitate, as that could imply something misleading. We mustn't misunderstand this as merely having will power to tame unruly schedules! Make no mistake friends—overwork is a *spiritual* issue, tangled up in our insecurities and fears, desires for accomplishment and recognition. It is only as we make the choice to abide in Jesus, strengthening ourselves spiritually, that we will be able to resist the temptation to work at a pace we can't sustain.

I'm learning, step by step, to live into this, and I'm learning it primarily by watching how Jesus went about his ministry.

FOLLOWING JESUS' LIFE (NOT JUST HIS TEACHING)

A few years back I heard a speaker point out, "We are committed to studying and learning from what Jesus taught, but do we also take time to study how he lived and learn from his practice?"

Overwork is a spiritual issue, tangled up in our insecurities and fears, desires for accomplishment and recognition.

This question caused me to see for the first time the very intentional pace at which Jesus lived.

This pace of life was captured beautifully for me by Dallas Willard, when talking with a pastor about how one would describe Jesus in a single word. The word Dallas chose was *relaxed*.[2]

Relaxed? Really? It fits, once I stop to think about it, but it is far from the first word I would have reached for were the question posed to me. As I reflect further, I realize I probably don't see it fitting Jesus because I don't see it fitting me.

Jesus never seems to be in a hurry.

This in spite of the fact that all four Gospels portray his ministry as full of crowds that overflow houses and hillsides, whose desire to be with him trumps their needs for hunger or shelter, and who manage to reach him even when he's on vacation. Jesus is peppered with interruptions from needy people, even as he is on his way to tend to other needy people. His life is busy.

Yet Jesus never comes off as rushed. One gets the impression that he perpetually lives at a walking pace—what Alan Fadling refers to as the "pace of grace"—even though immersed in a swirl of chaotic busyness.[3]

He is calm, relaxed, even-keeled—even in a squall that his fishermen disciples regarded as life-threatening.

> One day Jesus said to his disciples, "Let us go over to the other side of the lake." So they got into a boat and set out. As they sailed, he fell asleep. A squall came down on the lake, so that the boat was being swamped, and they were in great danger.
>
> The disciples went and woke him, saying, "Master, Master, we're going to drown!"
>
> He got up and rebuked the wind and the raging waters; the storm subsided, and all was calm. (Lk 8:22-24)

Here is, perhaps, the quintessential picture of Jesus as relaxed—comfortably enjoying a nap while the disciples are panicked. A professor of mine had a wonderful acronym for this: nap as *non-anxious presence*—a quality he saw as essential to spiritual leadership. In fact, Professor Walling liked to define a leader as a "self-defined person with a non-anxious presence."[4]

A self-defined person: not swayed by public opinion, the latest shift in the cultural winds, or the pressure to conform to what the consumers of religious goods and services decide they want on any particular day. They hold a deep, stable assurance of who they truly are, as defined by the Father.

With a non-anxious presence: unrattled by circumstances, quietly confident, because they are not the product of the crowd's opinions of them, nor victim to the storms that leaders must navigate. They trust that whatever comes, the Lord is their shepherd, and they therefore lack nothing. Relaxed.

It's a portrait of leadership I've been prayerfully aspiring to since the day I heard it, and it's also a perfect portrait of Jesus. He is the Father's beloved Son, secure, delighted in, and called for a purpose. You, too, friend, are the Father's beloved son or daughter, secure, delighted in, and called for a purpose. This—not your ministry—defines you, and forms the basis for you to live and lead as a self-defined person with a non-anxious presence.

Jesus' response to his disciples is as simple as it is instructive:

"Where is your faith?" he asked his disciples.

In fear and amazement they asked one another, "Who is this? He commands even the winds and the water, and they obey him." (Lk 8:25)

The disciples respond like I so often do in a crisis. "Ruin! Destruction! It's over!" Jesus rebukes the wind and waves, but not the disciples. Instead he poses a question, which I hear as a gentle one, meant to provoke honest reflection: *"Where is your faith?"* Is it in your ability to muscle through a violent storm, or in the One whom even the winds and water obey?

This is the core issue, isn't it? Where *is* my faith? If it is in my own need to beat back the storms that buffet my church plant, all I can do is motor faster and hope to outrun the weather. It's only if our faith is in the one who controls all things that we will have freedom to live at a non-anxious pace.

"For the follower of Jesus, the world is a perfectly safe place to be," I once heard Willard say. If we are in the kingdom, secure in the Father's love, what can truly harm us? Not even death is to be feared. And indeed, when death came for Willard, he didn't seem the least bit afraid. He was safe in the kingdom on this side of death, and knew he would be safe in the kingdom come on the other side.

This is how Jesus led, and how he wants to teach us to lead. The goal is that we might say, "I live not at the mercy of the culture's pace, but blessed by the mercy of an unhurried Savior."[5]

PACE-SAVING DISCIPLINES

In a church plant, how do we do that? How do we find a sustainable pace that will promote health in us, our families, and our churches?

There are several practices in Jesus' life that I see again and again in healthy church planters.

Silence and solitude.

> Very early in the morning, while it was still dark, Jesus got up, left the house and went off to a solitary place, where he prayed. (Mk 1:35)

> But Jesus often withdrew to lonely places and prayed. (Lk 5:16)

With these words the Gospels describe the first incidence of what the disciples will learn is Jesus' regular practice. Indeed, it was the regular practice of Jesus to get away for solitary prayer before entering into a time of ministry (Mk 6:30-31), after times of ministry (Mk 6:45-46), when receiving guidance (Mk 1:35-39), before making important decisions (Lk 6:12-16), and to be strengthened in times of distress (Mk 14:32-35). I would argue, in fact, that the pursuit of solitary time with the Father might be Jesus' core spiritual discipline.

Solitude with the Father grounded him, refueled him, and gave him what he needed to lead at the pace of grace. And it is not meant to be unique to him—Jesus invites his disciples into this same rhythm of life as well:

> Then, because so many people were coming and going that they did not even have a chance to eat, he said to them, "Come with me by yourselves to a quiet place and get some rest." (Mk 6:31)

Every planter will find themselves in a place where so many people are coming and going that you don't even have time to care for your basic needs. Jesus' response to this situation is surprisingly counterintuitive. The wise church planter who wants to live long in the land will respond to these seasons, not by increasing their speed to keep up with demand, but by saying yes to Jesus' invitation to solitude. "Come with me, by yourselves, to a quiet place, and get some rest."

The practice of solitude looks different for everyone, but I like to think about my practice in terms of daily, monthly, and yearly rhythms.

Solitude with the Father grounded Jesus, refueled him, and gave him what he needed to lead at the pace of grace.

My daily routine begins in the early morning before the family is up, my inbox is open, or I've looked at my phone, as once I've begun chipping away at the day's tasks, I have a hard time settling into a deep enough quiet to really be fully attentive to God.[6] My regular post is at the kitchen table with a steaming cup of coffee and my Bible, journal, and perhaps a spiritual book, where I can watch out the window as the neighborhood awakens. There, I spend time with Jesus as he speaks to me through the Word and the Spirit, and as I bring him my questions, concerns, and requests about what the coming day will bring.

The time is rarely magical, but I find there is a comfortable closeness that comes with consistently meeting Jesus in this way, day after day, week after week, year after year. I'm nourished by it in deep, quiet ways, such that if I miss this time, it's like I've missed a meal.

I find that this simple act of beginning my day alone with Jesus is foundational to keeping him in the front of my mind, and receiving what I need from him for that day's tasks and interactions as the day goes on.

In addition to this daily rhythm, on the first day of every month a reminder pops up in my calendar to schedule my monthly day of solitude. The reminder prompts me to look over my calendar and figure out which week is most conducive to one less work day (my arrangement with my church is that they treat these solitude days as work days), and to lock it in before that day has a chance to be overrun with appointments or other work. I find that if I don't literally put these days on my calendar, they won't happen.

Typically, on solitude days I try to get an early start. I live close enough to the beach that I will sometimes go there, or to one of a couple of very serene nearby parks. I find a shady spot to set up a chair, and (again) armed with a thermos of coffee, I read and pray my way through the morning. On solitude days, the longer time frame creates space for the Spirit to get to deeper places than in the half hour or so in my daily rhythm. In longer solitude, there is more space for the Spirit to unearth areas in my soul that need care, or for a Scripture text that seems to be vying for my attention to drill its ways through my defenses.

And while a countless number of God-driven insights about ministry or myself have come on these days, most days are not about getting some profound message from God. Most days what I need is just to be still, and be reminded that I'm God's child. I need silence and solitude for that to happen.

It's important to me to make space for joy in these days too. Ordinarily, when I've tired of sitting, I will go for a run (I enjoy that), as I find that some of my best praying happens when I run. And I like to combine these days with what Richard Foster calls the "discipline of celebration," which basically is doing nice things for yourself, in God's presence, as an act of worship.[7] So at lunch I'll try to splurge a little and treat myself to something I really enjoy.

In the last hour or two of my afternoon before returning home, I'll open my inbox and respond to anything that needs immediate attention. Then, if at all possible, I go home a little early, and break my fast from people by being with my family.

Finally, once a year I drive a couple hours to a camp in the local mountains that makes their speaker's cabin available to pastors looking to get away with God. There I take a twenty-four-hour prayer retreat, which follows much the same pattern as my daily and monthly solitude times, just longer and richer. This yearly rhythm has a way of clearing a path for God to speak graces and truths to those parts of my soul that especially need it.[8]

Again, most of my times with God are not especially magical, but when I stop and look back, I can see there is an unmistakable pattern of God using these times to bring me closer to him. Our spiritual formation seems to come a drop at a time—a cumulative drip, drip, drip that happens in us as day after day, month after month, year after year we create space to be with our Savior.

Sabbath-keeping. We could be forgiven for forgetting that Jesus was committed to observing the Sabbath, as almost every mention the Gospels make about the Sabbath involves accusations that Jesus was breaking it. Yet . . .

> He went to Nazareth, where he had been brought up, and on the Sabbath day he went into the synagogue, *as was his custom.* (Lk 4:16)

As an observant Jew, Sabbath-keeping was part and parcel of what it meant to faithfully worship God. Far from disregarding Sabbath, Jesus was committed to keeping it, and doing so in ways that preserved its intent. And much to the chagrin of his opponents, he was unconcerned with maintaining any unhelpful trappings that had grown up around it over time.

He summarized, "The Sabbath was made for man, not man for the Sabbath" (Mark 2:27). Sabbath is a gift to us, Jesus says. It is part of how God intends to give us abundant life.

Many times when I've taught the creation story, I've said that creation reaches its culmination when God created men and women in his image (Gen 1:26-27). And while it's true that creating humankind was the pinnacle of God's *work*, it is not the full story. God's creation actually culminates with God's *rest*.

> Then God blessed the seventh day and made it holy, because on it he rested from all the work of creating that he had done. (Gen 2:3)

The Sabbath, we're told, is holy because on that day God rested from the work he had done.

I find that pastors in general, and church planters in particular, have a hard time with this. How can I rest when there is still work to do? Good, important, meaningful work? But we have to remember that God not only blessed the *work* we would do (Gen 1:28) but also the *rest* we would take (Gen 2:3). In fact, the Sabbath goes a step beyond blessing: "The good is the base, the holy is the summit. Things created in six days He considered *good*, the seventh day He made *holy*."[9]

Hopefully you have some sense that the work you are doing—gathering a congregation to worship God and disciple themselves to him—is holy work. But friend, do you recognize that your rest from that work is also holy? That there is a sacredness to the cessation of work as well as its engagement?

When I find myself unable to turn off the work instinct, I'm reminded of the Deuteronomic account of the Ten Commandments. Exodus and Deuteronomy use almost identical language as they prescribe the Sabbath—until they get to the Sabbath's rationale. At that point the two tellings take different paths.

In Exodus, the writer offers the Genesis account as the basis for Sabbath-keeping—that built into the rhythm of creation is a blessed, holy day when God rested (Ex 20:11). Therefore we, too, like the God in whose image we are made, must keep Sabbath. That we were made to operate according to a particular rhythm, and that ignoring that rhythm is perilous, is crucial for us to remember.

But in Deuteronomy there is no mention of creation. Rather, we find a second, equally important rationale:

> Remember that you were slaves in Egypt and that the LORD your God brought you out of there with a mighty hand and an outstretched arm. Therefore the LORD your God has commanded you to observe the Sabbath day. (Deut 5:15)

Remember, God says, *there was a time when you didn't get to rest. You were slaves, who had no choice in the matter. But I've saved you from that—now you are free! You no longer have to be enslaved to your work.*

Yet so often we are.

Pastors become slaves when we feel we need to say yes to every request, to satisfy every need presented to us, and when we live in fear of failure, or of disappointing those we serve. We are slaves when we believe the heretical lie that this holy work we do is dependent on our unceasing expenditure of energy, rather than on the unlimited energy of Jesus, the true head of the church we serve. That we dare not stop, because then what would happen to the church?

And that lie is a sneaky one, because the image of an overworked pastor seems on the surface to be a picture of unselfish servanthood. Many in our churches are happy to reward us for this with recognition and admiration. But that picture is an illusion. You are *not* being a sacrificial servant by neglecting sabbath for yourself. You are neglecting God's wisdom, and in doing so are being selfish. A burned-out shell of a pastor does no one any good.

How do we unlearn this frantic way of pastoring and replace it with a non-anxious one? We keep sabbath. Sabbath is not a burden for us to keep, but God's gift meant to keep *us*. It keeps us from making ourselves into slaves when we don't have to be.

Many pastors take Monday as their sabbath, but I take Fridays. I find that on Mondays my mind races with a cascading list of to-dos prompted by the events of Sunday. My attempts to rest on Mondays are continually interrupted by my overactive mind. I relax better on Fridays, plus, Fridays let me take two days off in a row (usually). I try to keep these days simple and have been greatly helped by Eugene Peterson's maxim that sabbath is a time to "pray and play"—a day when we don't try to accomplish anything, but simply spend unhurried time in the presence of God and others we love.[10]

Someone looking in from the outside might be surprised at just how unspiritual my sabbath looks—maybe even less spiritual than my other days. A lot of praying happens, but it is more in the course of slowly making my way through the day. On Fridays I go buy groceries. I take a walk with my wife or bike ride with my daughters. I watch YouTube, read articles that have nothing to do with church, and geek out on my hobbies. Like I do on my solitude days, I might treat myself to a food I enjoy or have a little nicer wine with my dinner. All this is done in the presence of God, as an act of grateful worship.

And part of the beauty of sabbath is that it doesn't stop with that one day, but teaches us how to keep healthy rhythms of work and rest, wake and sleep, engagement and disengagement in the other six days as well. Or as Wayne Mueller sagely puts it, "Sabbath dissolves the artificial urgency of our days, because it liberates us from the need to be finished."[11]

BECKY LAHNA, *LEAD PASTOR OF GOODLAND CHURCH, SANTA BARBARA*

Heading into the planting endeavor, I had to assess the burnout and spiritual exhaustion I was experiencing in the seventeen years of ministry prior. I was exhausted! I knew that something in my style of leadership needed to change in order to create a sustainable and life-giving rhythm for my leadership. In my quest to be healthy and still be me, I discovered three shifts that have helped immensely.

First, I had to change the way I thought about goal setting. I am a driven, goal-oriented, fast-paced person. I like big challenges, and I have a high level of energy to spend. Within the context of church planting, most of the time success is measured by numbers because, well, numbers are measurable. But just counting heads doesn't mean you are measuring the right things. So instead of creating a goal around how many people I would have attending activities at different points in time, I made a goal to meet three people a day. It's a goal that pressed me into motion and mission, while also allowing me the freedom to put the results in God's hands. As a goal-oriented person, I needed goals that formed my soul in a life-giving way.

Another shift was making space for others to lead. As a church planter, I find it easy to settle into the mindset of work harder and work more for God's glory (and perhaps, if I'm being honest, my own glory and success). My drive to succeed pushes me to make things happen. But just because I *can* make things happen does not mean that I *should*. So I am learning how to make intentional choices about what I will not do, in order to create space for other people to lead. This practice means I have to either wait until the right person comes along or intentionally raise up someone else to lead. Both options are difficult for me (they slow me down), but they are building within me a healthy dependency on God.

As an example, I had been leading musical worship in our Sunday evening house gatherings, so when we made plans to have a more traditional Easter service at the beach our first year, I ended up leading everything—the music, service, and preaching. As a result, I did nothing excellently. Everything was mediocre, at best. I felt deeply disappointed. This year was a different story. Our core team began preparing for Easter much earlier, and I repeatedly said that if we were going to do another service, I was not going to lead the music. So we prayed and waited together. I invested in a couple of musicians and slowly began giving them more leadership. Now we have a team of people who own the musical part of worship. And they are much better musicians than I am.

The last shift was thinking about my own spiritual formation before the formation of the church. Entering into this season of ministry, I have dug in my heels and stubbornly refused to plant this church out of anything other than an intimate relationship with Jesus. Strategy and plans are necessary, but a growing relationship with Jesus was essential for me, the planter. Consequently, we adopted a goal of being self-feeding disciples of Jesus who reproduce self-feeding disciples. That meant, by necessity, that if I did not have a growing relationship with Jesus, there was no way I could reproduce a disciple who had a growing relationship with Jesus. This commitment forced me to make tactical decisions about the ways I spent time with people, as well as what structures we chose to put in place. The result? A greater emphasis around the practice of spiritual disciplines together and engaging in activities that show love for our neighbors.

Cultivating joy. I once heard an interviewer ask *Late Night* host David Letterman if he was a happy person. He said his happiness came in twenty-four-hour increments, based on how the previous night's show had gone. A lot of pastors operate the same way. Our happiness is tied to how Sunday went, or whether the congregant we are counseling felt helped, or whether that visiting couple returns a second time.

If we haven't found an undercurrent of joy that runs deeper than our week-to-week triumphs and failures, we will certainly be worn out within our first few years.

But woe to us if we go into the roller coaster of church planting with our happiness tied to our win-loss record! Soaring highs and crushing lows come with the territory. If we haven't found an undercurrent of joy that runs deeper than our week-to-week triumphs and failures, we will certainly be worn out within our first few years. Cultivating joy is indispensable to a sustainable pace.

I suspect much of this is tied to how we see God. Do we see Jesus as joyful?

Of course Jesus was all about the work of the kingdom, but if we see him going about this with grim seriousness rather than lightness and joy, then we will certainly take ourselves and our work too seriously too.

We must not forget that this was a man who made time to enjoy meals with friends, attended a friend's wedding (and apparently could tell a good wine from a mediocre one!), and delighted in children. His opponents apparently found him suspiciously happy, as they accused him of eating and drinking too much, like the questionable sorts at the parties he attended. *Why don't his disciples get somber-faced and fast twice a week like we do?* Jesus' answer offers a clue to his demeanor. They can fast later, he says. Right now they are with me, and that makes this a time for joy (Lk 5:33-35).

And why not? "In your presence," the psalmist says, "is fullness of joy" (Ps 16:11 ESV), and Jesus prays that his followers "might have the full measure of *my* joy within them" (Jn 17:13). Dallas Willard is certainly correct when he says of God that "undoubtably he is the most joyful being in the universe."[12]

Do we believe this? That Jesus ministers from a place of joy, and can teach us to do so as well?

What is it that brings you joy? What might Jesus use to cultivate in you a deeper capacity for joy that transcends circumstances? I find that life-giving time playing with friends is essential (this is, by the way, the first thing that gets squeezed out when I'm overly busy). My days are full of a lot of serious conversation, so I need to be intentional to create spaces where laughter can happen.

Exercise, with its life-giving endorphins and physiological release of bodily stress, is also a nonnegotiable factor for me in cultivating joy. In fact, exercise is on my short list of spiritual disciplines I believe every planter needs in their rule of life.

Meals with my family. Listening to my daughters talk about their day. Sitting on the couch with my wife, talking about nothing, or everything, or just watching television. Practicing gratitude. Re-reading notes of gratitude of those I've served (I actually keep an encouragement file on my computer).

These small acts, so easily neglected or omitted in the busyness of life, are life-giving. I'm learning to consciously invite Jesus into them, asking him to use these to make my inner life more like his inner life—joyful, peaceful, non-anxious.

One final note. As I was writing this chapter, I got an unexpected lesson in joy from a friend who has reached black belt status in its cultivation. I had flown to Seattle to visit David, a pastor friend who is battling pancreatic cancer. It's been a while since we've been together, and I was taken aback by how different he looked. His once-famous hair was replaced by stubble, his muscular frame now uncomfortably thin. Throughout his ordeal, the need to cultivate joy in the midst of pain has been a well-trafficked aspect of our conversations.

Lately David had been in and out of the hospital, and it pains him not knowing from one day to the next how well he will be able to serve the church he loves. While visiting, I was going to help out by preaching and by meeting with his leadership team to help them process a difficult issue they're facing.

I'll spare you the details, but I woke in the night and noticed something in my body wasn't quite right. As a precaution I went to urgent care, who promptly sent me to the ER. I still didn't really think anything was wrong until the doctor came in and started talking about my test results. I listened for a full minute before I really heard her. "Wait, are you saying you're admitting me to the hospital?" I asked, dumbfounded, as my mind raced through the commitments I'd made, which I might not be able to keep. "That I'm not leaving right now?"

The doctor looked at me like I hadn't been paying attention. "You aren't leaving this hospital *for several days*," she replied.

I called David to tell him what was happening, and to say how sorry I was that I wouldn't be able to meet with his team or speak on Sunday. He told me how sorry he was I was sick, assured me the church would be fine, and then got quiet.

"So what you're telling me," he said, a smile creeping into his voice, "is that the pastor we brought up because I'm too sick to preach is in the hospital?" And like the two old friends that we are, we laughed hard, having had a small taste of that joy that runs deeper than circumstance.

FOR REFLECTION AND DISCUSSION

1. Do you consider silence and solitude an easy discipline or a difficult one? In either case, what benefits have you received from spending quiet time with God?

2. Do you have a set day for sabbath? What does sabbath-keeping look like for you?

3. What brings you joy? What can you do to create space for more joy-inducing activity in the presence of Jesus?

FURTHER RESOURCES

An Unhurried Leader by Alan Fadling
Invitation to Solitude and Silence by Ruth Haley Barton
The Sabbath by Abraham Heschel

8

TEAM

Have I Relinquished My Ambition to Be a Superhero?

Control is the Sacred Cow of established churches, and it needs to be ground into gourmet hamburger.

WILLIAM EASUM

What you are doing is not good.

JETHRO, SPEAKING TO MOSES (EXODUS 18:17)

"IF YOU AREN'T GOING TO LEAN ON US FOR SOMETHING LIKE THIS, THEN WHY ARE WE EVEN HERE?"

Ron's face was red, visibly pained, his hands tightly grasping the air in front of him as each word punctured the room's silence.

It was the only time I had ever seen Ron angry. Or, to be more precise, it was the only time I had seen any expression of emotion from this stoic, northern European, mechanical engineer. "Seriously," he continued, "you *have* to let us carry these things with you." He gestured toward the others in the room—the dedicated lay people that comprised our college ministry's volunteer staff.

"You aren't going to make it in ministry if you don't learn how to lean on your team," he concluded somberly. Other leaders around the room nodded. Another added, "That's right, Tim."

The incident that precipitated the outburst? I was a young staff pastor serving college students, when one night a young man approached me after a message I had given. At first I thought he was going to say something complimentary, as he liked to do, but as he got closer I could see by his face it was something else. It turns out I had quoted an author who had recently become the target of this young man's favorite radio apologist. He was convinced that the author was a heretic, and since I thought enough of the author to quote him, I was too.

Thinking the situation could be resolved through reason, I set a meeting with the young man. I clarified what I believed, showed him from where in Scripture my beliefs were derived, and explained where I did and didn't agree with the author in question. But the young man was not having it. I was dangerous and needed to be removed from ministry before I could infect others. By the time the situation was finally resolved, he had met with our senior pastor and various elders to call for my firing, and since they did not act quickly enough, had prepared a mass mailing to the congregation to let them know of my unsuitability for ministry.

What started as almost humorous grew into something that kept me up at night and really took an emotional toll on me. (This being the first time someone made it their ambition to end my ministry, I didn't have muscles for it. Unfortunately, I've had opportunity to get a little better at it over the years.) It was only then that I let the team know, which is what bothered Ron.

Part of me wanted to respond to Ron with my rationale, which seemed solid at the time. I didn't want to sully this young man, who really was a good guy, albeit deeply troubled. *I can just ride this out*, I thought. I was wrong, and the lesson of that event stuck with me.

When we started Life Cov, I knew my approach had to be different. In our first leadership meeting, I told our new team, "One of the things I need from you is help carrying those parts of ministry that drain me, and especially to help me when I come under personal attack."

Over the years, our team has been amazing in this. When someone's gripe with the church gets centered on me, they are quick to say,
"We've got this from here. You just worry about doing your job." In
fact, recently we went through a protracted season of difficulty with
a congregant that devolved into some pretty rough personal attacks
against me. It's a situation we haven't been able to share freely with
the congregation, which has made it tougher still as that cuts across
our values. One night during a leadership meeting, I heard myself
saying to them, "When I reach retirement age, if I'm fortunate enough
to still be a pastor, it's going to be in large part because of you."

HOW TO WEAR OUT YOURSELF AND THOSE YOU LEAD

It's not unusual for church planters to function like superheroes—to
see ourselves as self-sufficient, independent, and more capable and
knowledgeable than we actually are. Armed with a calling and backed
by the Holy Spirit we fearlessly lead, heal, save, and inspire. We swoop
in—strong, knowledgeable, and impervious to danger—share the
plan, motivate people into action, and bask in the glory when glory
results. But slow down, Paul says to the superhero pastor. "Do not
think of yourself more highly than you ought" (Rom 12:4).

In one way or another, every chapter in this book addresses this
question, but here I want to specifically turn our attention to the
question of how we utilize teams. A passage that continues to teach
me in this is the story of Moses experiencing near exhaustion in the
midst of ministry, and his healing encounter with his father-in-law,
Jethro (Ex 18:1-27).

The passage opens with a detail, given almost as an aside, that
should jar awake anyone in leadership:

After Moses had sent away his wife Zipporah, his father-in-law
Jethro received her and her two sons. (v. 2-3)

He sent his family away? Though we aren't explicitly told, the passage
seems to connect this fact to the workload the passage describes as it

continues. It would seem Moses had a hard time doing both ministry and family well.

I can't read this passage without asking myself, *Are there times when I have sent my family away?*

There are seasons in our church's life when, looking back, I think the answer may have been yes. I was physically present but not really there. I let myself become too busy, or too preoccupied, or work more hours than I should have, and there simply wasn't enough of me left to be emotionally present once I got home. The work was too important, you see, and demanded all of me. So, though we shared a house, my loved ones—my first and primary ministry—had, in effect, been sent away.

As we continue reading, it's important to note that Moses was not lacking for results:

> Moses told his father-in-law about everything the LORD had done to Pharaoh and the Egyptians for Israel's sake and about all the hardships they had met along the way and how the LORD had saved them. Jethro was delighted to hear about all the good things the LORD had done. (vv. 8-9)

There was much to celebrate! And they did—Moses and his father-in-law enjoyed a meal and raised a glass to how good God had been: rescuing them from Egypt and preserving them as, impossibly, this enormous mass of humanity had made their way through the wilderness.

Nearly all planters fear failure, but not enough fear success.

But I have to wonder if that wasn't part of the problem. God kept showing up, and they kept getting results, so that means everything was good, right? Moses' ministry was fruitful, so what could be wrong?

As church planters, we need to note and celebrate the fruit God brings, but that cannot be our only data point. God is gracious, and it's surprising how often we see his blessing remain on a ministry even when we are not heeding his hand guiding us toward better health. But in addition to the fruit, we have to look at the cost and ask some hard questions. Is the work becoming more than I can bear? Are there any negative effects on my church? On my family? Is this sustainable?

Nearly all planters fear failure, but not enough fear success. Results have a way of blinding us to problems we desperately need to see.

After a night of celebrating, Jethro went to work with Moses, to see what a typical day on the job looked like.

> The next day Moses took his seat to serve as judge for the people, and they stood around him from morning till evening. When his father-in-law saw all that Moses was doing for the people, he said, "What is this you are doing for the people? Why do you alone sit as judge, while all these people stand around you from morning till evening?"
>
> Moses answered him, "Because the people come to me to seek God's will. Whenever they have a dispute, it is brought to me, and I decide between the parties and inform them of God's decrees and instructions." (vv. 13-16)

Moses' proverbial schedule and inbox were full—a throng of people with their problems and disputes, swarming around him from sunup to sundown. Why, Jethro had to know, are you doing this?

Moses answered in much the same way as any of us who feel God's call. *The people need me. God has called me. So I do it, even though I'm about to drop dead.*

Moses is operating like he is a superhero. Jethro is about to remind him that he is not.

> Moses' father-in-law replied, "What you are doing is not good. You and these people who come to you will only wear your-selves out. The work is too heavy for you; you cannot handle it alone." (vv. 17-18)

This isn't good, Moses. You will wear out, and so will those you lead.

Most pastors, when we take on more work than we should, do so primarily from a place of selflessness. *Why should I trouble someone else with something so mundane? I'll just do it myself.* We determine it is better to do a bit more ourselves, and get worn down a little, than to put it on others and see them get worn down.

But this passage reminds us of a truth that is so easy to forget: both we *and* those we lead will get worn out if we are doing more than we should. What on the surface looks like selflessness is in fact selfish! Doing it all is *not* the best thing for us or for those we lead.

If we do more than we should and consequently wear out ourselves and those around us, are we really doing what is best for our people? Not to mention that if we are doing it all, we rob others from the blessing of serving God as well. Whatever the motive, when you do more than what you should, you do a disservice to yourself, those you lead, and the family you risk sending away.

Jethro's solution is as simple as it is wise: *Do the things God has called you to do, and empower others to do what God has called them to do.* Jethro says,

> Listen now to me and I will give you some advice, and may God be with you. You must be the people's representative before God and bring their disputes to him. Teach them his decrees and instructions, and show them the way they are to live and how they are to behave. (vv. 19-20)

This is Moses' portion of the work—that thing that he must take responsibility for. He has three tasks: to represent the people to God, teach them what God wants, and show them what following God looks like in practice. *This is your job, Moses. Stay in your lane.*

Then comes part two:

> But select capable men from all the people—men who fear God, trustworthy men who hate dishonest gain—and appoint them

as officials over thousands, hundreds, fifties and tens. Have them serve as judges for the people at all times, but have them bring every difficult case to you; the simple cases they can decide themselves. That will make your load lighter, because they will share it with you. If you do this and God so commands, you will be able to stand the strain, and all these people will go home satisfied. (vv. 19-23)

Moses, you are not the only one who can lead. God has given you others who are wise to judge. Empower them to do it. And the result will be good: your load will be bearable, and rather than getting worn out, the people will go home satisfied.

Part of me reads this and says, "Of course—delegation! Leadership development! Simple, right?" But then another, quieter part of me speaks up and asks, "Why hadn't this happened already?" Not because it's complicated. Jethro didn't waltz in and give a lesson in nuclear physics—he gave Moses an org chart.

And here is where the passage gets uncomfortably personal as I wonder what kind of internal struggle Moses had at this point. *What? Trust others to judge these cases? Sure, we've got some good people, but this following God stuff is serious business. Do these others have as much wisdom as me? Do they know God's laws like I do? None of them were on the mountain with me. Do they have the same kind of closeness with God that I have? I don't see any of them being called "God's friend."*

And just like that, I'm exposed. The difficulty is more than structuring the ministry properly. This is a problem in me—a spiritual problem. It would seem I trust God to act through me but not through others. Which is the same as saying that I trust *me*, not God. Perhaps I think I'm a superhero.

MOVING FROM SUPERHEROES TO EQUIPPERS

What we see in seed form with Moses, we see as a fully grown paradigm in the New Testament church. In Acts 2 we learn that the Spirit has now been poured out on all believers. They are gifted and empowered to serve, and many will be called to lead.

The apostles find that they can't tend to the ministry of prayer and the Word and at the same time ensure that food is distributed fairly among the widows. So they tell the congregation, "Choose seven men from among you who are known to be full of the Spirit and wisdom" (Acts 6:3).

When Paul sends Timothy to Ephesus and Titus to Crete, he is explicit that they are not there to be supermen who will do it all themselves. No, he gives them a list of character traits and ministry competencies, and tells them to select leaders—elders and deacons—who will be empowered by the Spirit to serve the churches. And Paul not only preaches this, he lives it. His letters are sprinkled with praise for valued coworkers and names of regional leaders Paul commends to the churches, and nearly every letter ends with words of thanks and greeting to the women and men who give leadership in the various churches.

But perhaps Paul's clearest articulation of this principle comes in the job description given in Ephesians 4:

> Now these are the gifts Christ gave to the church: the apostles, the prophets, the evangelists, and the pastors and teachers. Their responsibility is to equip God's people to do his work and build up the church, the body of Christ. (Eph 4:11-12 NLT)

Jesus gave leaders to the church as a gift—not as those who would do the work for the people, but as those who would equip the people to do the work.

Put another way, if you as pastor are doing the bulk of ministry, then you are pastoring wrong. The pastor's job, Paul tells us, is not to do the work of ministry but to raise up a church that does the work of ministry.

The pastor's job, Paul tells us, is not to do the work of ministry but to raise up a church that does the work of ministry.

So from day one—literally—the church planter must begin to give away ministry to those they lead.

But here is the rub, as most of us will immediately recognize. To be an Ephesians 4 pastor, to be Moses-post-Jethro, requires more than simple structural changes. It requires heart change as well. How do we develop the spiritual competencies required to give ministry away to others? Four practices stand out to me in church planters I've seen do this well.

FIGURE OUT WHAT KIND OF PASTOR YOU ARE SUPPOSED TO BE

Before I can fruitfully utilize those around me, I need to be clear about who I am.

Moses may have been too close to see it, but Jethro was able to articulate, "These are the things that you, Moses, need to do: represent the people, teach God's word, model a godly life." Boom.

What does such a simple assessment do? The beauty is that it not only tells the leader what to focus on but also gives them freedom to *not* focus on everything else. Clarity in our role is an essential precursor to empowering others in theirs.

I find that many church planters stop too soon in exploring their call. Yes, they feel called into planting, and perhaps that has been confirmed through an assessment or a denomination or network extending a call. But we have to go the next step and ask, *What kind of planter am I called to be?* I'm not just talking about your job description, but of the core gifting God has given you, through which you will shepherd and lead.

My friend John is an evangelist. Everything he does comes out as evangelism. He might be inviting you to dinner, but by the end of the invitation, he will somehow be inviting you to salvation as well. And even though you are already saved, he is so compelling that you might get saved again. He pastors as an evangelist, because at his core, that is who he is.

My friend Peter is a prophet. You might be conversing about the weather or baseball, but somehow the conversation will pivot, he will expose and name a societal injustice, and you will suddenly find yourself part of a group he has organized to do something about it. Peter pastors with a strong prophetic bent—it is who he is.

Doug is a gatherer—a virtual party waiting to happen! He pastors from a place of joy, laughter, and community. Scott is a chaplain—he pastors best when he can walk into a room and sit down right in the middle of people's pain. Camille is a preacher's preacher—weaving the text, poignant stories, and her own life into a perfect tapestry, all delivered with a polish and cadence that makes it impossible to look away.

I am a pastor-teacher. I am at my best when my energy goes into studying the Bible and teaching the church how to apply it in ways that help them grow up big and strong in Jesus. These are the gifts through which I lead.

What kind of pastor are you? And what do you do with this knowledge once you have it?

For starters, we need to do what we can to shape our days around activities which help us lead out of who we are.

Bob Logan, a seminal voice in the world of church planting, recommends a simple practice for new planters that helps them clarify their role. Make a thorough list of everything (everything!) that you need to do. Don't leave anything off—make it as comprehensive as possible. When the list is complete, go back and put a star on those tasks that *only you* can do. For *every other item*, write the name of someone else from your core team that might be able to do that thing. Then, take your first twenty minutes of every workday delegating these tasks and following up with those assigned to them.[1] The goal is to get to a place where roughly 80 percent of your work time is spent doing things that you should be doing. Not only does this free you up to be as fruitful as possible, but it instills in your church's ethos a high value for serving.

REDUCE THE LAYERS OF "NO"

Longtime church consultant Bill Easum used to think that the core hang-up preventing most churches from moving forward was resistance to change. But while this theory made sense when he asked churches to give up something that was dear to them, it didn't explain the resistance when he asked them to add a new ministry. Why resist, he wondered, when you don't actually have to give up anything? Eventually, he came to the conclusion that it wasn't change that was the issue, but control. As churches mature, he concluded, their appetite to keep order increases, and their tolerance for risk decreases. He memorably writes, "Control is the Sacred Cow of established churches, and it needs to be ground into gourmet hamburger."[2]

One of the biggest barriers to becoming an Ephesians 4 pastor is a culture of control. Controlling environments serve to disempower the body from using their gifts for the good of the church and the world.

This came home to me some years ago when I was a staff pastor at a large, well-established church. I was part of a working group that was tasked with figuring out why, in a church with so many financial and people resources, it was so difficult to get the congregation to serve. We identified a number of factors, but the one that made the biggest impression on me was the many layers of "no" a person had to navigate if they wanted to start something new.

It looked like this. Suppose a person in my area of ministry wanted to start a new ministry, say, to provide food for impoverished people in nearby government housing. That person would come to me, pitch the idea, and I would say, "Yes, this is great." Except I would first need to go to my supervisor and make sure he was also good with the idea. If he liked it, we would take it to a committee that oversaw our area of ministry. If they approved it, the chair of the committee would present it to the elder board. If the elders liked it, we would ask the senior pastor. If he also liked it, then I could go back to my congregant and tell them to go for it.

The process was inefficient and time-consuming, which discouraged many people from even trying (or others just chose to bypass the system altogether and not ask permission). But worse yet was the fact that so many people received rejections for ideas that seemed to be no-brainers.

Why was this? For a given ministry to go forward, it needed to receive five yeses, but only one no would shut the whole process down! And inside of a culture that tended toward order and self-protection, the chances that one of the five people whose approval was needed would find something that could go wrong was pretty high. Is it any wonder that over time our church developed a culture of non-volunteerism? Every leader would state emphatically that they wanted to be a church where people were empowered to serve out of their giftedness, but our systems unintentionally created a highly disempowering dynamic.

By contrast, Easum recommends reducing the number of decision-making bodies in the church down to one, or at most two—a practice we employed when we started Life Cov. At Life Cov, we have

A little mess is a small price to pay for a church where a lot of good things happen because the norm is for people to serve.

our vision team (pastors and elders) and our frontlines team (small group and ministry team leaders). (These are teams, not committees, meaning that they are actually serving in the areas they lead, as opposed to a board that makes decisions for others to follow.)

Our rule of thumb is that the closer one is to the actual ministry, the more of the decisions they should make. This clarifies the vision team's role as one of broad, thirty-thousand-foot-level oversight, not micromanagement. And it empowers frontline leaders to have broad authority within Life Cov's vision and values to shape their teams, launch new initiatives, and set their own budget as they need in order to accomplish the work to which they are called.

"Doesn't it get messy," I'm sometimes asked, "not exercising more control over the church's ministries?" Sure, at times it can, but in reality, not very often. For us, a little mess is a small price to pay for a church where a lot of good things happen because the norm is for people to serve. (More than 80 percent of our people are in identifiable ministry roles.)

G. K. Chesterton summed up this philosophy beautifully when he wrote, "The more I considered Christianity, the more I have found that while it had established a rule and order, the chief aim of that order was to give room for good things to run wild."[3]

BE AMBITIOUS FOR THOSE AROUND YOU

To the extent we can, we've attempted to make every ministry in the church team-based, such that there is no area where only one person is able to perform a given task. A brilliant practice that we picked up early on has helped immensely with this.[4] When a person is looking to start a given ministry, we ask two questions. The first is, Who will do it with you? If you can find two or three others who want to share in this, then great, you're now a ministry team. The second question is just as important: When will you take your first day off?

This question does two things. First, it communicates a message we find easy to state but harder to show: *you are more important than what you do.* Second, it means you as a ministry team leader have to teach someone else to do what you do.

We regard burning people out to be a serious sin, and a failure of leadership on our part. As such, no one should be the only person who is able to perform a given task, such that if you get sick, go on vacation, have a baby, and so on, that thing can't get done. Putting these two questions to new prospective leaders has gone a long way in creating a healthy ethos of servanthood, and has also given us a natural pipeline for identifying and training up new leaders within existing teams.

So where does this practice get difficult? Not in terms of organization, but in terms of ego. Teaching others to do what you do means that you don't get to be a superhero. In fact, our encouragement to leaders is to be intentionally ambitious for those around you—look for those who will be able to do it better than you do. This came home to me as we were putting this into practice for our worship gatherings. If we were asking every other team to operate in this way, then we needed to take a team approach to teaching and preaching the Bible, right?

Don't get me wrong—I wanted to take a team approach. I knew intellectually that I certainly wouldn't be the only person in the church gifted to teach, that our church would benefit from a diversity of voices in the pulpit, and even that I would be a much better pastor if every three or four weeks I was able to work on other things because I wasn't preparing a message.

But I was scared. *What if the church likes the other teachers more than me? What is my value as pastor of this church if I am not its best teacher?* Swallowing this fear and doing what I knew was best for the church required a lot of prayer and the occasional pep talk from those near me. And even though this process has now been repeated many times, it continues to challenge me every time we have brought a lay person or new staff member into the teaching rotation.

The biggest challenge, though, came just a couple years ago. I had an opportunity to bring an amazing new staff pastor into the church, who I knew would be a life-giving partner for me, and who brought a wealth of gifts to the church. The only problem? He's a better preacher than I am. It is one thing to *wonder* if someone else would be a better Bible teacher than me, but could I tame my insecurities enough to *intentionally* bring in someone who would outshine me in one of my primary areas of giftedness?

God helping me, I did, and it's been amazing for the church and for me. When we are ambitious for those around us, the church wins, and it helps wean us from the compulsion to be the church's superhero.

MAKE SURE YOUR LEADERSHIP TEAM HAS AUTHORITY (NOT JUST A TITLE)

For many pastors, and especially church planters, we operate with more of a Moses (pre-Jethro) model of ministry than a New Testament model. Like Moses, we go to the mountain, receive a vision from God, and then go to the people and tell them what to do. Our authority is near absolute, and input from others is an optional extra.

By contrast, in the New Testament we never find a solo, Moses-like pastor. Instead, we find that authority is entrusted to a plurality of discerning, spiritually maturing, capable servants who will exercise leadership together.[5] One or more of these servants, in our modern structuring of the church, we might hire and call "pastor." But we should be clear that in biblical parlance that person would still be a member of that church's leadership team.

This model is easy to see in the Scriptures, but in the form modern churches typically take, it can be difficult to exercise in practice (and more so in traditions that really elevate the role of pastor). And in a new church, where the planter often starts as a solo leader, we are even more susceptible to falling into a superhero-like, pastor-as-Moses model.

At Life Cov, we have done our best to structure ourselves in a way where other leaders are not merely advisors to the "real" leader (the pastor), but to make every effort to truly lead as a team. Granted, the bulk of day-to-day decisions fall to staff, as the church has hired us away from other pursuits so we might give our full attention to leading this church. But all of our macro decisions are made together.

Our vision team meets often—every two weeks, for two and half hours—to pray for the church and for each other, and to seek God's wisdom in leading our congregation. Most the team are laypeople with their own day jobs, so to maximize their capacity to give meaningful input, we try to look far enough ahead that we avoid rushed decisions. One can't foresee every crisis, but to the extent possible, we always want to have sufficient time to thoroughly discuss and prayerfully come to a consensus on a given issue.[6]

Like everyone else on the team, my voice is worth one vote. Yes, being the pastor, I'm sure it's fair to say I have more influence than others, but I have no more authority than any other team member. They can tell me, and have at times told me, "We respect the idea you are putting forward, but no, we don't collectively think that is how God is leading us." As much as I dislike this (*What do you mean my idea isn't brilliant?*), I need the chastening it brings. How can I be anything other than a superhero pastor if no one can veto me?

And while I have some input, I don't choose my team—the church does. Every year one or two team members rotate off, and others come on to take their place. There is a discernment process for this, which always begins with a question to the church: "In whom are you experiencing gifts of wisdom and leadership?" The church, not me, says who they want to lead them.

I end this chapter with a prayer I find myself returning to often, as this pastor strikes me as one who had both a clear sense of his role, and a high view of the church under his care.

> Now you have called me, Lord, by the hand of your bishop to minister to your people. I do not know why you have done so, for you alone know that. Lord, lighten the heavy burden of the sins through which I have seriously transgressed. Purify my mind and heart. Like a shining lamp, lead me along the straight path. When I open my mouth, tell me what I should say. By the fiery tongue of your Spirit make my own tongue ready. Stay with me always and keep me in your sight.

Lead me to pastures, Lord, and graze there with me. Do not let my heart lean either to the right or to the left, but let your good Spirit guide me along the straight path. Whatever I do, let it be in accordance with your will, now until the end. And you, church, are a most excellent assembly, the noble summit of perfect purity, whose assistance comes from God. You, in whom God lives, receive now from us an exposition of the faith that is free from error, to strengthen the church, just as our fathers handed it down to us. (John of Damascus, ca. 645-754)[7]

FIL AND JUANA NESTA, *COPLANTERS, LA JORNADA*

We were new church planters, just six months into the process, when the senior pastor of a sister church plant announced that he was moving. This plant was several years old, and the news of his departure came out of nowhere. Everyone was shocked, including us. We were asked if we would be willing to merge our church plant with this established church. We thought it was an answer to prayer.

At the time, our church already had sixty people and was meeting weekly. They were a strong group, but far too much of the work of ministry was falling on the two of us. Not to mention that in our particular Latino/Spanish church context, making our budget was a real challenge, and an influx of people would really help.

By contrast, the church that we were merging with had a little over two hundred people, an associate pastor, and a complete leadership team! We thought we were going to grow in attendance and leadership bandwidth, because two hundred plus sixty equals 260, right? Wrong! We didn't know that the church we were merging with was riddled with internal conflict.

On a cold winter night in October, we met with the leaders of this new church, who we thought would be added to our existing church to create a dream team. This actually turned out to be one of the most discouraging experiences of our ministry walk as church planters. We still remember sitting at the table with high hopes and our vision presentation, ready to take over the city and beyond for Jesus. But before we could even power up our laptop, one by one those leaders turned in letters of resignation. By the time everyone was done, we looked at each other in panic and disbelief. I looked at Juana and said, "So where does this leave us?" She answered, "We now have no worship leader, children's leader, youth group leader, men's leader, women's leader, or associate pastor."

When the members of the church realized that their beloved pastor and leaders were leaving, they left as well. We quickly realized that without a team, the hope of having a church of 260 went out the door. All at once we were back at square one, with the same sixty people we had brought into the merger.

The experience was painful, but the lesson that came out of it was priceless. Prior to this, we as church planters did everything. *Everything!* But having for a brief moment been faced with the prospect of pastoring a church four times the size, we realized that wasn't sustainable—particularly if we saw ourselves pastoring a larger church as time went on. We recognized that developing a strong team of leaders was not optional but *essential* to having a healthy church plant.

And the surprising good news: once we developed and trained our homegrown leaders, many of those people that left returned. We became a thriving Latino church—with a great team of leaders.

FOR REFLECTION AND DISCUSSION

1. Looking honestly at your approach to leadership, to what extent would you say you are in danger of "sending your family [and friends] away"?

2. What are your core giftings? What percentage of the time would you say you are leading through these? What practical step might help you increase that percentage?

3. On a scale of one to ten, how easy would you say it is for someone in your church to start a new ministry? Are there unnecessary barriers that could be eliminated?

4. Are you willing to share your authority? To mutually submit yourself to a team of leaders? What structural changes might be needed to make this happen?

FURTHER RESOURCES

Called by Mark Labberton
Let Your Life Speak by Parker Palmer
Pursuing God's Will Together by Ruth Haley Barton
Sacred Cows Make Gourmet Burgers by Bill Easum

CONFLICT

Do I Handle Difficult People Graciously?

Saint Francis walked the world like the pardon of God.

G. K. CHESTERTON

*The Lord's servant must not be quarrelsome, but must
be kind to everyone, able to teach, not resentful.*

PAUL TO TIMOTHY (2 TIMOTHY 2:24)

"I FEEL LIKE I NEED TO SAY SOMETHING YOU MIGHT NOT
WANT TO HEAR."

I took a deep breath before continuing. The couple on our couch
was having marriage problems. Big, gnarly, this-thing-is-about-to-
come-crashing-down problems. They had been married less than a
year. Our church had existed for less than three months. They were
one of three young married couples in crisis.

"Whenever our conversation comes around to areas where your
actions might be contributing to your difficulties, you get defensive,
and shift the conversation back to what your husband is doing wrong."

Her head moved back a little in shock, her jaw stiffening with
anger. She started to reply, then stopped herself. Then, her jaw loos-
ening, she smiled sweetly as her expression moved from anger to pity.

"Well," she said, "I certainly don't think I'm perfect, but I'm not sure you understand what it's really like living with my husband."

"That's the other thing," I continued. "We've noticed in your story a recurring pattern. Whenever people in your life suggest that you may be part of the problem, you reject them. You have a number of therapists and pastors in your past that you left because you concluded they were incompetent, as well as friends that you have cut off, and even family members that you won't talk to anymore."

My wife chimed in at this point. "In fact, we're concerned that in bringing this up, this might be the last conversation we have—that you might decide that we are incompetent too and move to another church. But we're really hoping that this will be different, and that you will let us walk with you in this."

She smiled, laughed, and assured us that no, she wasn't going anywhere. But they had barely gotten to the car before she told her husband it was time for them to find a church with more qualified leadership.

Where two or three are gathered, there will be conflict, as anyone in church leadership knows. And while it's difficult to marshal data to support this claim, anecdotally it would seem that church plants *Where two or three are gathered, there will be conflict.* have a way of attracting an even greater amount of conflict than an established church. Dealing effectively with this requires the church planter to develop a specific set of ministry skills. But by this, I don't just mean techniques. It requires God to do a work in us, developing us to a place where we become spiritually competent to engage people with his grace.

THE THREE "HIGHLYS"

Dave Olson was the longtime national director of church planting for the Evangelical Covenant Church. Under his leadership, church planting had flourished, both in the number of churches planted, and at an unprecedented rate of success. When he spoke, church planters would take out a pen and start taking notes.

"Among those who are attracted to being part of a new church," Dave offered, "you will find three kinds of 'highly' people: the highly missional, the highly needy, and the highly controlling." Each of these, he went on to explain, would require you to have direct, sometimes difficult, conversations.

Highly missional. The highly missional, Dave explained, are believers who hear about what you are doing and feel called to help make it happen. Often these people are mature Christians who feel God stirring them to do more for the kingdom, and they are restless as they wait for him to show them what that might be.

When we find that we have gained a highly missional person, we do well to invest ourselves in them and help them find their place in the body. They are with you because they want to change the world, and what they need is to know their contribution matters—that they are, in fact, changing the world. It's true, and they need to hear it validated by their pastor. And we do right to ask a lot of them—to serve, to give, to invest in those less mature in the faith.

"These people are a gift! Invest in them, as some of these will become your first leaders," Dave said. "But," he cautioned, "even as great as these people can be, there is still a hard conversation that has to happen."

He went on to remind us that we plant churches to reach the unchurched, not to take people from other churches—a fact that can be easy to forget when we find ourselves face to face with a mature believer who loves our vision and wants to get involved. We need to serve them and our church well by asking, Is God really calling them to this? Have they talked to the pastor of their current church? Is there anything at that church they are running from? If things seem questionable, sometimes it is best to send them back to their previous church.

Highly needy. The next "highly" is the highly needy person. This person is wounded and desperately needs someone to minister to them. At times their need is overt, but often it starts hidden and shows itself gradually. When they hear about your new church, they are filled with hope that this may be a church where (finally!) their longings will be fulfilled. But as their woundedness begins to display itself, we discover that their road to healing can take a tremendous amount of time and attention.

It's common to hear in their stories that they have been part of a number of churches, and those stories frequently end with this or that church or church leader letting them down. It is easy, hearing the depth of their pain, to forget that we are only hearing one side of the story. We might express admiration for their resilience, and unwittingly buy into the hero worship they direct our way, assuring them that yes, we are in fact going to be different from all those that came before us. We will be that church that loves them well, and where they find what they have been longing for.

"But be careful," Dave cautioned. If we slow down and listen between the lines, overlaying their story with how we are experiencing this person, we might begin to wonder if their bad church experiences came, not because their previous pastors were incompetent, but because this person wore their previous pastors out! That the level of care they required was more than a mere mortal could provide. "Keep in mind that a day may be coming when this person will be sitting with another pastor telling them about their last pastor who let them down—you!"

When the church planter finds they have a highly needy person, we do well first to give thanks. Here in front of us in an opportunity for the church to be the church! Why else did we begin this work, but to see lost people saved and hurting people helped? This person can be a tremendous gift, and to see a person come into the church wounded, and then heal over time, is like oxygen to a pastor's soul and nourishment to the collective body.

At the same time, we have to recognize that without good boundaries, a pastor could easily spend all of their time and energy on this person. Consequently, other people and other responsibilities get neglected, we become frustrated, and eventually we might come to resent rather than shepherd this person. We need to exercise wisdom, lest over time we find ourselves worn out by the insatiability of this person's needs, and like those before us, become exasperated with them. One of the worst things we could do would be to add to their wounds by losing patience and lashing out.

We have to be generous with our time, no question—but we also serve them and our churches best by setting good boundaries, and in so doing, teaching them how to be a good community member. If we are going to serve this person well, we must have clarity about what we can and cannot do for them, arm ourselves with gentle yet forthright honesty, and make clear that we cannot be their sole caregiver. We enlist the help of other believers, bring mentors alongside, and make sure this person gets into a small group.

Such measures might strike them (and us, if we aren't mindful) as selfish. But this is not selfishness—it is good pastoral care. We are protecting them, in a sense, from wearing out their welcome among their church members and exasperating their pastor. Setting such boundaries, and being courageously honest about what is required of this person, is difficult for us to do and difficult for them to receive. But it is a gift, and we must love them enough to give this gift.

Highly controlling. Finally, church plants attract the highly controlling person. This person, like their highly needy counterpart, typically has been part of a number of churches. But where the highly needy person has stories of churches not meeting their needs, this person has stories of churches that don't know what it means to be the church. It typically doesn't take much digging to realize that they are very confident in their vision of what a church should be, and darn it all if these previous pastors just wouldn't take their good counsel to heart. Or alternately, sometimes this person had a particularly rich church experience ("Praise Chapel, back in 2010!"), and they have been trying to recreate this experience in every church ever since.

For the highly controlling person, a new church represents a fresh opportunity to make a church in their own image, and a fresh young pastor might be just pliable enough to embrace their ideas of the way things ought to be done.

For the church planter who discovers they have a highly controlling person, wisdom is required, seasoned with heavy doses of honesty and courage—because the controlling person is frequently an intimidating person to confront. Such a meeting need not be contentious, but a pastor must be absolutely clear on what their vision is, and ruthlessly specific in where their vision differs from that of their enthusiastic congregant. One must avoid the temptation to give false hope that in the future the church's vision might become what this person is hoping it will be. Clarity, not agreement, is the goal.

Once clarity is established, two paths emerge. If the congregant can accept your vision, you can work toward "agenda harmony" and the possibility of fruitful partnership. Can this person, despite different preferences, get behind what this church is doing?

The other path we refer to as "out-counseling." If the person simply can't get behind the vision God has given this plant, then the best thing you can do for them and for the health of your church is to help them find a church that better suits their needs. This is hard, particularly as in the new church it feels like you are fighting for every person you can get! But in having this kind of hard talk, you are giving a gift to that person, to your church, and to yourself.

Agenda harmony can happen, by the way. I have people in my church today who I was certain would opt out after having such a clarifying conversation, chalking us up as yet another church that didn't get it. Yet they came around and have become valuable contributors to the community. This too is a grace.

I can also recall times when I was too slow to out-counsel, as I could see the resource this person could potentially be to our rag-tag band of disciples, and I hoped against hope that I could convert them to my way of thinking. Without exception, when I made this mistake, it caused me pain and additional work as I had to stem the flow of their disgruntlement as it spread to others. Eventually (and in spite of my clinging to them), these people left the church anyway, but not before causing more harm.

Not having the difficult conversation with this person is ultimately selfish. I need to seek not only what is best for our church but also for this person. And I need to trust God as well, that if I let a person go who is a bad fit, God will bring another in their place.

A church planter can reasonably expect to have all of these difficult conversations in the first weeks and months of a new plant. But that, of course, is just the beginning. Pastoring well involves frequent uncomfortable conversations—some of which will be minor, and some of which will have very serious ramifications for that person and for the overall health of the church.

Not much can compare with conflict when it comes to revealing how we, at this moment, are doing in our own relationship with Christ.

So how do we do this well? How do we become people who are able to handle challenging people with courage and grace?

HOW PAUL HANDLED OPPOSITION

What encouragement would Paul give to a young pastor involved in the work of church planting in a highly secular environment? There is one passage in particular that has ministered deeply to me in this, when Paul attempts to prepare his young protégé, Timothy, for difficult conversations that he would need to have. His words highlight three areas of competency that we can ask Jesus to cultivate in us.

Character. Paul begins his instructions to Timothy, not so much with what to *do*, but with who the young pastor needs to *be*.

Flee the evil desires of youth and pursue righteousness, faith, love and peace, along with those who call on the Lord out of a pure heart. (2 Tim 2:22)

Forget about the difficult person in front of us—not much can compare with conflict when it comes to revealing how we, at this moment, are doing in our own relationship with Christ.

So, unsurprisingly, Paul begins here. "You," he says to Timothy, "need to be the kind of person who can fruitfully engage in conflict in the first place." So run away from—*flee*—any and all desires that aren't of God. And run full strength toward—*pursue*—virtues that reflect Christ: righteousness, faith, love, and peace.

Paul reminds the young pastor that before he sets out to bring correction to others, he needs to bring it to himself. This harkens back to the words of Jesus as well. Before you attempt to bring help to others, Jesus says, take care of the plank in your own eye (Mt 7:3-5). Without that, how will you see clearly enough to be a help to anyone else? Who we are always precedes what we do. So, the necessary precursor to dealing with difficult people is dealing with the difficult person we find in the mirror.

Paul further highlights this key issue by stating that Timothy's motivations must come from a deep place, a "pure heart." Think about it: if all we have to offer to others is a well-managed exterior, the best we can hope for is that others may experience an absence of harshness. But they need more than that—they need to encounter Jesus.

Therefore, there is one key question we need to ask: *Is my inner character becoming like the character of Jesus?* We do well to ask, *Am I spending time in his presence asking him to refine these things in me? Am I creating space to be with Jesus, and in that letting him do the slow, joyous, painful work of making me more like him?*

Your competency in graciously handling conflict is entirely related to your own apprenticeship to Jesus.

Wisdom. Like the call to character, Paul's next instruction also precedes any direct conversation we might have with a challenging person. It is a call to wisdom:

> Don't have anything to do with foolish and stupid arguments, because you know they produce quarrels. And the Lord's servant must not be quarrelsome. (2 Tim 2:23-24)

Without question, in both his teaching and example, Paul calls church leaders to proactively confront problems in the church. Sin, false teaching, those who would sow division in the body, and interpersonal dynamics that will erode the church's unity comprise a bare minimum of what a leader must proactively address.

Most of us will intuitively sense that there are two ways we can go wrong in this. We don't want to be avoiders, allowing unhealth to seep into our church's culture because our discomfort with conflict means we never address sin and unhealth. On the other hand, we don't want to just jump into confrontations unthinkingly, making everything a battle whether it needs to be or not.

That is why this verse, tucked into a section on confronting in a book that is all about confronting, is so important. "You don't need to engage with every argument," Paul seems to say. "Some are just stupid. They won't lead to greater health, just more fighting." As Paul elsewhere says to Timothy, we don't engage with arguments that aren't "advancing God's work" or promoting love within the body (1 Tim 1:3-5).

Like most people, I don't like conflict, so my most natural tendency is to avoid difficult conversations altogether. But as a new church planter, I began to experience the truth of what I'd been taught—that leaving bad behavior unaddressed can be disastrous. We are stewards of the church's culture, and if we are permissive toward behaviors and attitudes that cut against a Christlike culture, it causes real harm.

So I learned how to confront. But unfortunately, I lacked wisdom. I went from confronting as little as humanly possible to thinking everything needed to be confronted. The pendulum swung too far.

Not only was this exhausting, but it did little good for those I led. The leader who fights for nothing and the leader who fights over everything ultimately end up in the same place. In either case, their church learns nothing about what to value.

The key question we need to ask ourselves is, *Am I fighting the battles that are worth fighting?* Does this argument promote quarrels or love? Advance God's work or distract from it?

The battles you fight reveal what you truly value.

The battles you fight reveal what you truly value. In fact, there may be nothing that communicates more strongly to a congregation, "This is truly important," and consequently, nothing that has more shaping power for a church's ethos, than what they see their pastor is willing to go to the mat for.

Two contrasting stories from our church's origins come to mind. The first involved a young woman with a bombastic temper. Most of the time she was sweet and well liked, but in the face of any perceived slights, she would go nuclear—screaming and yelling, nasty voice-mails, accusations and name calling, trashing the person to anyone who would listen. When other leaders and I sat down with her and her husband to discuss this, the meetings were not received well. The others had wronged her, and she was insistent that her reactions were natural and appropriate.

The heart of our message to her went like this: "We understand that anger happens, and that's okay. But the way you are treating people when you are angry is not okay. We have an expectation of how people in this church will handle their difficulties with each other, and if you want to work toward that, we are happy to walk with you as you do so. But you need to know, we aren't going to tolerate the kind of behavior we keep seeing."

The woman opted to leave the church, loudly, and her friends were upset. "How dare you confront something so small as this? Don't you know that so and so is sleeping with their boyfriend, and that this other person gets drunk every weekend?"

Our response, I've come to believe, was very important in setting our church's DNA. "We are also sad that she chose to leave, but how we treat one another in Christ's church is not a minor thing. We aren't going to hesitate to call that out, as well as other sin areas, whenever it comes up."

The second story involves a young dating couple that got pregnant. They were embarrassed and repentant, but what, they wondered, is this going to be mean for our relationship with the church? Will we still be welcomed here?

"Look," I told them, "given that pregnancy isn't something you can hide, everyone is going to know about this pretty soon. Would you trust me enough to let us make it public together?" The next Sunday, the three of us stood before the congregation, and I shared about their pregnancy. "Like me and like each of you," I explained, "these two are sinners. The only difference is that you and I might be able to hide our sin, while theirs is a little more visible. And as I hope you and I do when we mess up, these two have owned their sin, are repentant, and doing what they can to walk in righteousness." People nodded and "amen-ed" their approval.

"What's more," I continued, "these two have a tough road in front of them, and they are going to need their church family to come alongside and help them as this baby comes into the world." And to my delight, the church did, from the baby shower they threw to the ongoing care for the family after their beautiful baby boy was born.

Now, I write this next part knowing not everyone will agree, but even if you disagree, think about what this communicates to the church. The end of my speech that day went like this: "Also, some of you know that Todd is a drummer, and he has been practicing with our worship team. In fact, it just so happens that today was scheduled to be his first day, and I, for one, am looking forward to being led in worship by him." With that, I took my seat, and Todd went to the drums.

Most of the church was fine with this, too, but there were some who were furious. "It sends the wrong message for someone who sins sexually to be in front of the church! You have to remove him."

I respectfully disagreed. "This is what grace looks like," I argued. "I'm not concerned about whether we would like to think a given sin is big or small, but whether the person is moving toward or away from Jesus—whether they are serious about sin, repentance, and righteousness. These two are, and that's enough for me."

People left over that incident. I didn't care. The way we manifested grace with one another was more important to me than the fallout. My willingness to fight for grace for this couple had enormous shaping power in our church.

Friends, the truth is, every battle you choose to fight, or choose not to fight, teaches the church what they should care about.

So the church planter who wants to handle conflict well must cultivate wisdom. Pray for it! It is one of the few prayers that the Bible explicitly tells us that God delights to answer (Jas 1:5). Regularly read Proverbs. Seek counsel constantly. Confer with your team. Get a mentor or coach, and listen to them.

By the way, that beautiful baby boy is now a teenager, and not too long ago I had the privilege of baptizing him like I baptized his father many years ago. And in a beautiful coincidence, the baptism took place at the beach, just a few yards from where I married his parents.

Gentleness. Finally, after we have addressed the matter of our own character and have used wisdom about whether the battle before us is worth fighting, we come to exactly how Timothy is to confront those who need to be confronted. And we find the heart of Paul's command is that Timothy be . . . *gentle.*

And the Lord's servant must not be quarrelsome but must be
kind to everyone, able to teach, not resentful. Opponents must
be gently instructed, in the hope that God will grant them repentance leading them to a knowledge of the truth, and that
they will come to their senses and escape from the trap of the
devil, who has taken them captive to do his will. (2 Tim 2:24-26)

Whenever I've taught this passage to pastors, I can't help but ask
with a twinkle in my eye, "Isn't it great to know Jesus agrees with you
that your opponents are tools of the devil?" The line always gets a good
laugh, but in reality Paul's intent is to stir up something we need if we
are going to do conflict well: *compassion*. Yes, there are times when
our opponents are in fact doing the devil's work. But most of them
don't know it. They have fallen into his trap and are now his captives.

I've learned that in the heat of conflict, when my emotions are
clouding my thinking, I'm helped by asking, *Is this person driven by
wickedness or weakness?*[1] I find that if I can manage enough emotional separation to honestly ask that question, an overwhelming
majority of the time the answer is weakness. Most of the time, the
person who is causing me so much frustration is doing the best they
can, and they typically think what they are doing is the right thing.
What does the pastor do with this?

Hopefully this knowledge helps us to live into Paul's words to be
kind and not resentful. It helps us to pray—not that the person would
go away, but that they would see the truth, change course, find
freedom, and be blessed. Hopefully it can move us to pray, "Father
forgive them, they don't know what they are doing."

Moreover, it helps me to ask the key question, *Am I treating this
person like a* person? A beautiful son or daughter of God, made in his
image, loved by him, for whom Christ died? Do I treat them with
dignity, respect, and honor?

But how are they not seeing this? another part of me wonders, exasperated. And Paul reminds me, it's because they don't know the

truth. *Well, they should know,* I fire back. And Paul says, No, don't just expect them to know. *You* need to teach them, and do so without resentment—kindly, gently. Such gentleness, John Stott writes, "is *the fundamental characteristic of the 'Lord's servant.'"²*

Gently instruct, gently instruct, gently instruct . . . This has become almost a mantra for me. Don't get angry or frustrated that they don't get it. They are ignorant of the truth, not because they are horrible people, but because they haven't taken the same journey that I have. It's by the grace of God that I know what I know. So gently and patiently teach them what they need to know, and pray God puts them in a heart space where they can receive it, and that they might move from a place of being oppositional to a place of freedom.

I don't pretend this is easy. Few things drain me more than oppositional people. But the way of Jesus is a gentle way. He would not break a bruised reed or snuff out a smoldering wick. I must not either.

WHEN NEGOTIATIONS FAIL

But what do we do when gentle instruction doesn't work?

Once, in the midst of a serious conflict, I felt paralyzed. I could see the person in question was causing harm to the body, but I knew a confrontation was going to lead to escalating drama with this person and those close to them. In the midst of my angst, a veteran pastor gave me this analogy. "A church's leadership is like the body's immune system. When infection threatens the body's health, antibodies come around that infection and contain it so it can't spread, and then move it out of the body. That's the role of the leaders too. They come around an area of unhealth and prevent its spread. And if that person won't be healed, they move it out of the body."

Won't be healed? *Who doesn't want to be healed?,* I wonder in these situations. But then I remember this lament of Jesus that my spiritual director likes to keep in front of me:

> Jerusalem, Jerusalem, you who kill the prophets and stone those
> sent to you, how often I have longed to gather your children
> together, as a hen gathers her chicks under her wings, and *you
> were not willing.* (Mt 23:37)

Jesus, too, had to weep over those who refused to change course and
find abundant life. Sadly, there will always be those who are unwilling
to be healed.

A new church plant, like a new baby, is by definition fragile. We
need to protect its health by proactively addressing whatever might
bring it harm. This is why Paul tells another of his protégés, "Warn a
divisive person once, and then warn them a second time. After that,
have nothing to do with them" (Titus 3:10).

Typically, a person so warned will correct course, or if not, they
will self-select out of the church. Only once in over two decades of
pastoring have we had to tell someone they had to leave. Should you
find yourself in that spot, make sure to utilize your team. If ever there
was a time for collective wisdom, this is it. Don't let your emotionally
charged perceptions rule the day—get others speaking into the situation! The decision to remove someone should always be a collective
one, never yours alone.

TONY GERVASE, *VISION TEAM MEMBER AT LIFE COVENANT CHURCH*

Imagine a top-ranked boxer headed through a crowded arena
toward the ring. Throngs of spectators are trying to get close to
him. Security guards hold back the crowds. A team of support
personnel flank him on all sides. There's his trainer, a manager,
and maybe a doctor or a coach as well. Key friends might be at
his side and certainly a bodyguard or two. All of these people
escort him down the aisle to the ring. They're tasked with his
safety and seeing that he performs at his best.

Your church's leadership team needs to be like the prizefighter's entourage, not only in seasons of church harmony, but most important, in situations of conflict. It's crucial that they are walking alongside you, helping you get through each battle in one piece. You don't want to be a pastor who is face down on the canvas every time there is a difficult church situation.

This is in no way meant to put you as pastor on a pedestal—I'm assuming you already know it's not all about you. This is just being real. Conflict is one form the spiritual battle will take, and it is meant to wear you down or take you out. And if you as pastor are not at your best, that will negatively affect the church.

I grew up in the faith and have attended churches both large and small. I recently concluded a lengthy, eye-opening, and rewarding stint on Life Cov's leadership team. I say eye-opening because this was a season where we witnessed our share of conflict. As one who doesn't create a lot of conflict, I didn't know that such times of strife could be so prevalent inside the church.

Below are some tips that flow out of our team's experience on how you as pastor can utilize your team to strengthen and protect you as you go through the battles.

Prayer. Just as it's important to pray for godly conflict resolution, make sure there are people praying for you personally during these situations too. A great time to cultivate this is when you meet with your team. Be honest about how you are doing, and ask them to pray for what you need. And don't forget to send periodic updates between meetings as well.

Prayer 2.0. If you are married, ask for prayer for your spouse too. Sometimes it's even harder for the spouse to see their partner under attack than it is for the pastor.

Don't do conflict solo. When you meet with someone with whom there is conflict, make sure at least one other person from your team is with you. Having a witness to the conversation prevents against mischaracterizations later.

Check-ins. Make sure you have someone on the team who will call, text, or email you regularly during the time you are processing the difficult situation. If you don't have a person on the team who will do this on his or her own, appoint one.

Be real. During the check-ins, honestly describe how you're doing. Your team can't help you if you are not honest with them.

Rest well. Either during or right after a difficult situation, take a day off (one that you'd normally be working) in order to recharge. Get away. Go on a hike, get a massage, see a matinee, exercise, or take a day of solitude. Do whatever you love to do that feeds your body and gives life to your soul.

Empower your leaders to lead. Sometimes a challenging church member will be a recurring source of conflict. Consider having another member of your leadership team be the point of contact with that person. Let them carry that burden for you.

Take notes. Don't think of this as "keeping a record of wrongs." Instead, keep a file of every email and text, as well as notes from each face-to-face encounter. You never know when you'll need them, and you don't want to rely on your memory.

May the Lord bless you and strengthen you to grow as a loving, grace-filled pastor during times of conflict in your church.

I end this chapter with a prayer that our Orthodox brothers and sisters pray in the morning. It isn't meant for pastors per se, but I find it helps me keep my bearings in any difficult conversations the day may bring.

O Lord, grant me to greet the coming day in peace, help me in all things to rely upon your holy will. In every hour of the day reveal your will to me. Bless my dealings with all who surround me. Teach me to treat all that comes to me throughout the day with peace of soul and with firm conviction that your will governs all. In all my deeds and words, guide my thoughts and feelings. In unforeseen events, let me not forget that all are sent by you. Teach me to act firmly and wisely, without embittering and embarrassing others. Give me strength to bear the fatigue of the coming day with all that it shall bring. Direct my will, teach me to pray. And you, yourself, pray in me. Amen.[3]

FOR REFLECTION AND DISCUSSION

1. Have you had experiences with any of the three "highlys"? What was that like?

2. Paul asserts that before dealing with difficult people, we need to deal with ourselves. Revisit your rule of life and ask, *Am I actually practicing the disciplines I need in order to grow in Christlikeness? Moreover, am I meeting Jesus in these disciplines, and not just checking a box?*

3. What practices have you found help you cultivate wisdom? Help you cultivate gentleness?

FURTHER RESOURCES

Strengthening the Soul of Your Leadership by Ruth Haley Barton

Overcoming the Dark Side of Leadership by Gary McIntosh and Samuel Rima

The Living Church by John Stott

FAMILY

Am I Leading in a Way That Brings Life to Those Dearest to Me?

If someone were to ask your spouse and children what they love or hate about the ministry, what do you think they would say? And here's a harder question: how much of it would have to do with you and your priorities?

CAMERON LEE AND KURT FREDRICKSON

If anyone does not know how to manage his own family, how can he take care of God's church?

PAUL THE APOSTLE (1 TIMOTHY 3:5)

"IF YOU LOSE YOUR FAMILY, YOU LOSE YOUR MINISTRY TOO."
It was probably the fifth time Wayne had told me that, and like always, I nodded compliantly. I knew he was right, but there was so much work to be done. My inner dialogue would protest, *I know, but . . . the church needs to grow, I need to meet with that couple I hope to recruit, I need to be out meeting unchurched people.*

But my coach was not messing around. His most pointed questions were always around my work-family balance, and if he didn't fully trust my answer, he would call my wife and ask her how I was doing!

"I've seen too many church plants succeed at the cost of the family losing," he said. "And that cost is too high. Do you want your kids to grow up loving the church or resenting it? Do you want your wife to be happy she married a church planter or wishing your job was something else? Plant this church in a way that brings life to your family."

RECOGNIZING OUR MOST IMPORTANT CONGREGANTS

I'm told that at the beginning of each new class, legendary seminary professor Howard Hendricks would shock his students by declaring, "It would be a *sin* for some of you to get an 'A' in this class!"

"My classes require a lot of work," he would explain. "And many of you, in addition to your studies, are working other jobs or serving long hours in churches. On top of that, many of you are newly married, or have young children at home."

"If that's you," he would say, "then for you to neglect those most important relationships for the sake of your grade would be a sin! It would be better for you to get a 'B' than to put your grade before your family."

As church planters, we would be wise to apply the same counsel.

It is entirely possible that if we run without stopping, we might get an "A" in church planting, however you define that (rapid growth? conversions? community presence?). But in doing so we might fail miserably in family. That would be a tragedy, and yes, a sin.

Friend, if you have a spouse and children, they—not the church—are your most important congregants. To succeed at church but fail at family is to fail, period.

And while I'm deliberately talking a lot about family in this chapter, I believe we can say much the same thing for those who are single. While the relational commitments are of a different sort, whatever our most important relationships, we need to be faithful to honor the bonds we have with those friends and family who are dearest to us.

> *To succeed at church but fail at family is to fail, period.*

For as long as we've been a church, I send out an email each week to a handful of trusted intercessors. Most of the requests differ week to week, but one constant is asking people to pray that my kids would grow up loving Jesus *and* his church.

I'm sure I don't need to tell you how many pastor's kids grow up bitter. Some preacher's kids are angry at God, but more are angry at the church. Maybe they saw the church grind down their mom or dad with petty criticism, or ignore good boundaries their parent tried to establish, or crush their parents' spirits in petty squabbles and conflicts. Maybe they saw their parent get used up or go unappreciated for their hard work. Or perhaps they had improper expectations of the pastor's family—that the kids would be super-spiritual, or the spouse would fulfill some stereotype of what a pastor's wife or husband is supposed to do.

Churches are, by their very nature, messy. People are imperfect. They are in process, and no one in the church (pastor included) is yet who they are meant to be. That means it is important that we as pastors have, and communicate to our families, realistic and gracious expectations of the church as less-than-perfect people.

But it also means that you and I need to take responsibility for cultivating congregational conditions that will promote good health for our families. We have to take responsibility to establish healthy boundaries, forge proper expectations of what a pastor is and isn't, and define what a congregation should and shouldn't expect of a pastor's family. We cannot expect others to do this for us—the responsibility is ours.

And as in other areas we've discussed, this is an advantage that church planters have over established churches. You get to set the tone. You are able to instill a DNA in this body that says, "This is how we relate to a pastor and their family." But it won't just happen—we need to proactively shape the church's culture.

And, I would add, our spouse and our kids need to *see* us proactively shaping the church in this way. They need to know that they matter more. One of my goals as a pastor is that my life would scream to my family, "I love you more than I love this church!"

As much as I've been deeply blessed by A. W. Tozer, I'm haunted by the toll his ministry took on his wife and children—one of whom described his mother as a "single parent." After his death, Tozer's wife married a man named Leonard Odom. Once she was asked if she was happy in this new marriage. "I've never been happier," she said. "Aiden [Tozer] loved Jesus Christ, but Leonard Odom loves me." Tozer was a good and godly man whose life has had phenomenal impact, but his blind spot with his family caused that impact to come at tremendous cost.[1]

How can we do ministry in a way that brings life to our families? I want to offer several practices that I believe help us in managing a healthy relationship between our families and the church. But, as with the other areas we have discussed in this book, doing that will be a byproduct of the spiritual competencies God is forging in us. So, let's first turn to what the Scripture says about managing ourselves.

OWNING WHAT IS OURS TO OWN

Three times in the pastoral epistles, Paul gives a list of qualifications for church leaders, and in all three lists, Paul highlights the importance of a leader investing in their family.

Now the overseer is to be above reproach, faithful to his wife . . . He must manage his own family well and see that his children obey him, and he must do so in a manner worthy of full respect. (If anyone does not know how to manage his own family, how can he take care of God's church?) (1 Tim 3:2-6)

A deacon must be faithful to his wife and must manage his children and his household well. (1 Tim 3:12)

An elder must be blameless, faithful to his wife, a man whose children believe and are not open to the charge of being wild and disobedient. (Titus 1:6)

In all three passages, Paul emphasizes the importance of faithfulness in marriage. The elder is to be "faithful to his wife" (and by extension, a female pastor ought to be faithful to her husband).

Some older translations rendered this passage "husband of one wife," which was at times taken to mean that an elder was not a polygamist or had never been divorced. But the NIV and others capture the sense of this phrase much better in equating it with faithfulness, as it is an idiom that might be better rendered "a one-woman man." The church's leaders are not just to be married to the right number of people or married the right number of times. They are to be unwavering in their commitment to their spouse, with eyes only for her or him.[2]

In addition, in all three passages Paul describes the leader's children in a way that would suggest a parent who is active and intentional in their children's development.

Why is this? One reason Paul gives is that how a person manages their home is a good predictor of how they will manage the affairs of the church. But it seems to me there is more going on here, too, especially as not everything Paul mentions is within a parent's control.

Yes, we can be consistent and loving disciplinarians, but does that guarantee that our children will not be wild or disobedient? Or, can any of us actually *make* our children respect us? And who of us, much as we might pray for it and work toward it, can say whether or not our children will believe? Yes, we can play our part, but in all of these things, we are dealing with humans who have their own will and will make their own choices. And we all know very good Christian parents whose kids chose poorly despite excellent parenting.

So what, then, is Paul doing? I hear him saying that we need to live in such a way that our homes become places where Christ is seen, and in that, that our children are given the best possible environment in which to choose him. While we can't ultimately control whether our children will obey, respect, and believe, we do have some control over the kind of people we—their parents—are becoming.

SHOW AND TELL

As I think about our vocations as church planters and the unique de-
mands that vocation will put on our families, two areas emerge as particularly important: what we model and what we teach. Both of these
are embedded in the instructions which follow the Hebrew *shema*, the
confession of faith recited daily by faithful Jews throughout history.

> These commandments that I give you today are to be on your
> hearts. Impress them on your children. Talk about them when
> you sit at home and when you walk along the road, when you
> lie down and when you get up. Tie them as symbols on your
> hands and bind them on your foreheads. Write them on the
> doorframes of your houses and on your gates. (Deut 6:6-9)

The Hebrew vision of passing faith to the next generation is a holistic
one, both modeled and taught by parents to children, and all in a way
that weaves them into the fabric of everyday life.

Modeling. First, these commandments are to be "on your hearts." That is, they are to be *part* of the parent (v. 6). The believing parent is not simply re- citing cold truth or teaching correct doctrine, they are imparting something that they themselves embody.

The Fuller Youth Institute (FYI) has done the most extensive research to date of kids who grew up in church, and the factors which contribute to kids still being in church once they are adults. While FYI is quick to say that there is no silver bullet, they have found several consistent factors that show up prom- inently in kids whose faith follows them into adulthood. Of those factors, which do they say is most significant? *Parents who really live their faith.* Kids who grow up seeing real faith in their parents are more likely to have real faith themselves.[3]

> *The believing parent is not simply reciting cold truth or teaching correct doctrine, they are imparting something that they themselves embody.*

We can all probably think of people we know whose church persona and home persona look nothing alike. The home persona might be angry and demeaning, for instance, while the church persona is all smiles and hallelujahs. For the child growing up under this—and even more so if their parent is the pastor—such a faith is portrayed as being neither real nor important. It is merely a religious ornament.

As we've noted throughout this book, it is all too easy in the busyness of a new church plant for a pastor's own spiritual life to go on the back burner. We need to remember that this affects not only us but also our children. We do well to ask, *Am I living in a way that gives my children every reason to believe? Do they see the reality of Christ in me?* And though no parent can make a child respect them, we should ask, *Do I live in a way that would give them reason to respect me?*

Does this mean we have to be perfect? Certainly not, as FYI's research confirms. But it does mean that we must be cognizant that when we lack congruity between what we profess and what we live, our kids will see it. So, own your failures. Call yourself out. Apologize when you blow it.

As parents, we can't control every dumb thing a congregant might say to our children, but we can control who we are. We can, God helping us, be people of integrity who demonstrate continuity between who we portray ourselves to be and who we are when no one is looking. Our family will know the difference.

Teaching. In addition to modeling the faith, we see here that the faith is to be taught. Talk about these commandments, the Lord says, when you are walking, or sitting, or standing, or laying down (v. 7). In other words, teach your kids God's ways all the time, as you go through life.

This is the way I picture Jesus teaching. As he is walking along the road, he sees birds perched on the branches of a mustard tree. He turns to his disciples, points, and says, "Hey! You know what the kingdom of God is like?" Or Jesus sees a farmer scattering seed. He points and says, "Hey! You know what the Word of God is like?"

In the same way, we teach the faith to our children, not just in formal ways, but in brief words exchanged as we stand at the sink doing dishes together, or in between games on the Play Station, or as we go on a bike ride, or drive them to school, or tuck them into bed at night.

Reminders of God's words were to be all around the Hebrews, wherever they looked—on hands and foreheads, doorways and gates (vv. 8-9). In the same way, our kids need to see evidence of our faith all over our lives. Faith is meant to be fully integrated—not compartmentalized—and woven throughout the fabric of life.

I believe this is what our kids need to see—faith that is real, lived, and embodied. I want my kids to see me at the kitchen table in prayer in the mornings. I want them to see me loving and laughing with their mom. I want them to see me being patient with them when they are making me nuts. When I blow it, I want to apologize quickly, and let them see me receive grace from God and from them.

Our families are our nearest and most important mission field. As planters, we need to lead in a way that brings them life.

To that end, I want to offer several practices that I've found helpful myself or seen be helpful for others. All are simple, and maybe even things you would do intuitively. But just knowing them won't help us—we have to do them.

TAKE ADVANTAGE OF YOUR FLEXIBILITY

When I was a new church planter, we rented space for our worship gatherings from a church that was itself only about twenty years old. Sometimes I would be in the building during the week, and if Dean, the founding pastor, saw me, he would pull me into his office. He recalled their church's beginnings like they were yesterday. He always wanted to know what we were working on, and he always had some wisdom for me. It was all good, but the piece that has been most helpful for me is one he probably wouldn't even remember giving. It came when my first daughter was about to be born.

"You want to know how to raise great kids as a church planter?" he asked. I was all ears.

"You already know that you probably won't make as much money as most of the people in your church, so you may not to be able to give your kids everything that they give theirs. But one thing you will have that many others won't is *time*. As a church planter you work a lot, but you have more control over your schedule than most people do. Take full advantage of that flexibility! Make a point to be there for your kids as much as you can: drive them to school, go to every game and dance recital, be home for dinner every night. You have plenty of time to work before they get up or after they go to bed, so don't worry about taking time during the day to be present for them. And don't feel guilty about your church getting their money's worth from you—trust me, they will!"

It was a simple word, but it changed my life. I've made a point at each stage of my girls' lives to work early if I need to, or after bedtime, so that I can be there for things that are important to them. I schedule my meetings such that I'm home for dinner almost every night, and that I attend all their events. I've regularly volunteered at their schools, coached their soccer teams, and chaperoned field trips. And sometimes I work from home for no other reason than to be near them while they do their homework. I find being present in moments that might seem mundane, when taken cumulatively, give them an overall sense that I am *there*—with them, in their lives, seeing and responding to life as it happens.

When I started these practices, I thought my girls probably wouldn't realize the benefit they were receiving until they were grown and looking back in hindsight. But it is interesting, even now as young adolescents, that they see it. They are realizing not everyone's parents are around this much, and they appreciate it. It's been great to be able to tell them, "This is one of the ways our church cares for our family—they let me keep a really flexible schedule."

SET BOUNDARIES WITH YOUR FAMILY IN MIND

I was a full-time seminary student when I got my first job in ministry. It was a great position that afforded me significant responsibility and opportunity to use my gifts with our church's college group, all while being mentored into ministry by the college pastor, Chuck.

I was so excited to be doing meaningful kingdom work that I had no concept of boundaries. I would work long hours, teach one to two weekly large group meetings with our students, lead a Bible study, and meet with students one-on-one most of the other nights of the week. I said yes to every opportunity that came my way, whether I had time for it or not.

But Chuck was a good mentor, both in teaching me ministry and in teaching me to be healthy. He would pop into my office some days and ask, "How many hours have you worked this week?"

"I'm not really sure," was my usual answer.

"I've seen you here too much!" he would bark.

"But I have to finish the . . ." Chuck would never let me finish that sentence. "No you don't. What you need to do is rest. Go home and find something fun and unproductive to do."

So began my journey toward healthy boundaries in ministry.

Chief among these boundaries was the practice of sabbath-keeping, a concept that was utterly foreign to me at the time—and frankly sounded ludicrous. My life was so crazy busy and overcommitted that I would read assigned books at stoplights, and Chuck wanted me to reduce my available working time by a full day? To somehow find one seventh more time on my other days to do all that I needed to do?

But as this discipline slowly began to do its work in me, I found that somehow sabbath allowed me to do more, not less. Yes, I had to get used to having a full day of not working. But I came to find that when I was working, I was more present to God and others. My time had decreased, but somehow I was able to do more in the time I had. And because I had a hard cap on the amount of time I permitted myself to work, I began to learn what I should say yes to and what I should say no to. Sabbath-keeping taught me the crucial importance of boundaries—how to set them, and how to keep them.

Since getting married, and even more so since having children, I've come to realize that these boundaries are not just important for my health, but also for those I love.

Consequently, I'm always looking for small ways to practice this, like taking my email notification off my phone so I can be more present when I'm home (because, I've learned, I'm incapable of not checking the email when that little notification pops up), or in bigger ways, like limiting the total number of hours I will work in a given week, and the times when I will do so.

In particular, when it comes to doing ministry in the evenings, I hold it to one or two nights per week (and require this of our staff as well). For me, this includes a standing leadership meeting every other week, and for much of the year I lead a midweek large-group study. So, on some weeks that means I have one night a week to be available for pastoral counseling, and some weeks I have none.

The implication of this is that sometimes I have to say to people who only have evening availability, "I'd love to meet, but my slots are full this week. Can you do a week from Thursday?"

This has been a real growth area, as it's not easy for me to put off someone who is in need of my help (and limiting myself in this way does create a bit of margin should a true crisis emerge that I need to tend to). But I have to remind myself that when I say no to the church, I'm simultaneously saying yes to my wife and kids—my first and nearest mission field.

EAT DINNER TOGETHER

Annie Dillard writes, "How we spend our days is, of course, how we spend our lives. What we do with this hour, or that hour, is what we are doing. A schedule defends from chaos and whim. It is a net for catching days. It is a scaffolding on which a worker can stand and labor with both hands at sections of time."[4]

The small routines we build into our days and weeks end up being the things that shape us. This makes it infinitely worthwhile to ask the question, What routines am I building into our family's life that will give life, and allow us to invest in our spiritual formation?

As we've noted elsewhere, our spiritual formation happens less in the big moments where God zaps us with life change, and more in the steady, everyday, almost mundane habit of simply being in his presence. Our children's formation happens in the same way. The faith is more caught than taught, and developing simple habits that bring us together is part of being a Deuteronomy 6 parent. For us, a simple part of this is the dinner table.

The small routines we build into our days and weeks end up being the things that shape us.

I try to protect that time from meetings and other commitments as much as possible. Sometimes one of the girls (or one of us parents) will be out with a friend, or we will have one of their or our friends at our table, but all told we end up eating together at least five times a week.

Some families have very structured sorts of devotional practices, and we have at times too. But dinner is a constant. We don't usually bring any kind of overt spiritual agenda to the table. We just give thanks, eat, talk about our days, and laugh a lot. But just because it isn't planned doesn't mean God doesn't get talked about. He always does, sometimes as we recount how he may have shown up that day, and sometimes he isn't named but is there nonetheless in the values that are imparted as we talk about life and how we choose to live it.

Day after day, meal after meal, story after story, our faith is being imparted. We tell stories about our days—things we are proud of or ashamed of, situations we got right or got wrong, and all the while—drop by drop—our kids are being formed as we "walk along the road" (Deut 6:7).

USE YOUR VACATION TIME

One of the ongoing challenges of planting a church is that a new church is naturally dependent on the pastor, and there are frequently not a lot of other developed leaders to rely on. Consequently, the sentiment I hear from a lot of planters when it comes to vacation is, "I'll take time off when the church is a little more established—a bit more stable."

Friends, fight the temptation to put off caring for yourself and your family until your church is "ready."

"But the church can't handle me being away," we might say. The truth is, if the church is going to be healthy, it *needs* to handle you being away. They have the Holy Spirit, and they have gifts that need to be activated if the church is going to thrive. Your absence is a great time to utilize latent gifts of administration, pastoral care, teaching, and so forth that reside in the body.

Granted, all this is new, so the church might not feel they can do this. But the other side of that coin is *because* all this is new, you have a chance to teach them that this is important, and then take steps to help them succeed. The sooner you get this into the church's DNA, the better it is for the congregation, and the better it will be for you and your family.

In terms of worship, many planters will try to line up a guest speaker, and that is a fine choice. But you might consider having a lay leader in the church teach. Our church has loved when we do this. Even if their speaking gift is not as developed as yours, hearing a peer teach the Bible is exciting and powerful. Or you can have someone facilitate a time of people sharing what God is doing in their lives. These have been some of our most powerful times of worship, to the point that we build them into our calendar once or twice per year.

Regardless of what you do to make it happen, use your vacations. You need this, your family needs this, and even your church needs this.

Walk away. Trust that they too have the Spirit. Let them do it.

One final story as we bring this book to a close. A while back I was in the car with one of my daughters. She was looking out the window thoughtfully, chin resting on her palm. I was just about to ask what she was thinking when she offered this: "I think when I grow up, I want to be a youth pastor."

"Oh yeah?" I asked nonchalantly, trying not to jinx the moment by showing too much excitement. "Yeah," she said. "I think that would be a pretty cool thing for a person to do with their life."

"Yeah," I said. "It's really a privilege if you get to do something with your life that you know makes a difference."

Now I know, her being a young teenager, that she will likely change her mind twenty-seven times before she actually grows up and pursues a profession. But still, I couldn't help but smile as we drove. *If she thinks a pastor's life is one she might want, we must be doing at least some of this right*, I thought.

FOR THE CHURCH PLANTER'S SPOUSE: SAMANTHA MOREY,
LICENSED MARRIAGE AND FAMILY THERAPIST

While much of what has been written to the church planter can also be applied to the spouse, I believe that as spouses we are a unique breed and need to be seen, understood, and supported in our own post and calling. Below are several words of counsel just for the spouse.

First, know that there is no one-size-fits-all ministry spouse, so having a clear understanding of who you are and what role you play in this adventure is vital. Some are highly involved in the work of the church, while for others their most significant ministry will take place elsewhere (through their work, home, or another area of ministry), and their church involvement will be more modest. Either option is fine, provided you are using your gifts and living in your calling.

Half the challenge, though, is that people will try to define your role for you or impose their own expectations as to what they think you should be doing. But you, spouse, have the opportunity to be the keeper of your own role and to maintain it as *you* feel called, not as others believe you are called. Preventing others from defining your role takes courage, grit, and the frequent extension of grace—not only for these others, but also for ourselves, and at times for our spouse.

Second, whether you are serving on the frontlines with your church-planting spouse or watching the process from the next seat over, you are going to get hit with ministry shrapnel. Ministry hurts. Consequently, it is so important that you are equipped with a self-care toolkit of your own to help you navigate the often unexpected and painful course that you blaze. At minimum, this means having safe friends (usually outside of the church) to dump your raw and unedited feelings on, an intimate relationship with God, and an open, intentionally honest, conversational relationship with your spouse.

Finally, I have seen in myself (and in many spouses that have gone before me) a temptation to harbor bitterness or resentment. Sometimes this is related to the shrapnel, and at other times it simply reflects a need to disengage from the busyness of church life and do a bit less.

While of course we need to be people who are kind, approachable, and willing to love, we also need to accept the responsibility to address these dynamics and tend to them as needed. I find it helps to ask myself questions such as:

Do I need to streamline my ministry service and say "no" more?

Do I need to allow myself to not attend particular activities, and resist the guilt that ensues?

Do I need to serve in a different area that honors my gifts more appropriately?

Do I need to have a heart-to-heart conversation with my spouse about over-busyness or better boundaries?

Whatever it means, let me offer you permission to explore this and to make adjustments as needed. Caring for yourself in this way will be a gift to your spouse and to the church.

FOR REFLECTION AND DISCUSSION

1. Look over the four suggested practices in this chapter. Are there any of these you are not currently implementing that you could, either in part or in whole? What changes would you need to make in order for this to happen?

2. Don't just guess what your family needs. Put down the book, go sit down with your spouse or children, and ask them to give you three suggested changes to how you do ministry that they would find life-giving. Same thing if you are single—ask those dearest to you what changes to how you do ministry would breathe more life into your relationships.

3. What are the best ways for others to support you in these practices? Ask your coach (or your peer-mentoring group) to provide some gentle accountability, and give them some guidance on how to do so.

FURTHER RESOURCES

That Their Work Will Be a Joy by Cameron Lee and Kurt Fredrickson

Sacred Parenting: How Raising Children Shapes Our Souls by Gary Thomas

How We Love by Milan and Kay Yerkovich

CONCLUSION

As this book comes to a close, I would like to leave you with one further encouragement: as hard as the work we do can sometimes be, *what you are doing is vitally and eternally important.*

In one of the last books he wrote before passing away, Dallas Willard penned some words especially for pastors. I find myself returning to them again and again:

> The most important thing that is happening in your community is what is happening there under the administration of true pastors for Christ. If you, as a pastor do not believe that then you do not understand the dignity of what you are supposed to be doing. Whatever your situation, there is nothing more important on earth than to dwell in the knowledge of Christ and to bring that knowledge to others.[1]

Friend, do you understand the dignity and importance of what you are doing? That in the midst of all the busyness, the frustrations, the bumps and bruises, that you are engaged in holy, crucial work that the world desperately needs?

I am glad that you have answered the Lord's call and that you have started an outpost of the kingdom in your corner of the world where men, women, and children are coming to know and to follow the crucified, risen, and glorified Lord. Thank you for what you are doing.

So as you get back to that work, I pray that you may know and experience the love and grace of God himself—Father, Son, and Holy Spirit—at the deepest core of your being. I pray that through your life and your teaching others will come to know, follow, and enjoy him too. And I pray that you might do this work in such a way that it honors him and brings joy to you and those near you, and that you can hold fast to the knowledge that what you are doing carries eternal importance.

May God bless you as you serve him.

Matthew 6:33

ACKNOWLEDGMENTS

I AM SO VERY GRATEFUL for the great host of people who helped in forming me as a church planter and who have given me opportunities to work with other church planters.

Two in particular have had a shaping voice in my church planting journey: Wayne Carlson, who was my coach, and Dave Olson, who invited me into ministering to other planters as part of the Evangelical Covenant Church's national church planting team. Just to share what I've learned from these two would take another book.

Similarly, I'm grateful for the other members of the Covenant church planting team, including and especially the regional directors of church planting, all of whom have taught me so much and know far more about church planting than I ever will.

I also want to thank my fellow members of the church planting faculty and board at Fuller Theological Seminary, and especially our fearless leader, Len Tang. It's a privilege to teach in such a rich environment with such gifted scholar-practitioners.

I want to thank Life Covenant Church for being a great church. Being your pastor is one of the great joys of my life! I want to give special thanks to our past and present pastoral staff, vision team, and small group and ministry team members. Thank you not only for leading with me but also for being so unselfish with me. That you support me in teaching and writing—aspects of my calling which only indirectly benefit our church—says so much about who you are.

Thank you, Jon Boyd at IVP Academic, for your gentle, patient coaching throughout this project, and thank you to the church planters and network leaders who spoke into my outline and/or read this manuscript.

This book is dedicated to Chuck Price, who made me take a sabbath and threw me out of the office when I'd been there too long. You mentored me not only into ministry but also into pastoring in healthy, sustainable ways.

Finally, I'm so grateful to my family for their support and encouragement. My wife, Samantha, is so brave and so patient. Whatever the adventure has been, whatever difficulty has come, you have always said yes without hesitation. And my beautiful daughters, Abby and Hannah, bring me so much joy. You motivate me to be the kind of Christian I would want you to emulate, the kind of father and husband you can truly respect, and the kind of pastor I would want you to someday have.

"Thanks be to God for his indescribable gift!" (2 Cor 9:15).

NOTES

FOREWORD

[1]Statistics vary but the Pew Forum is a good place to start. See "Age Distribution," Religious Landscape Survey, www.pewforum.org/religious-landscape-study/age-distribution.

[2]Scott W. Sunquist, *Why Church? A Basic Introduction* (Downers Grove, IL: IVP Academic, 2019).

[3]Len Tang and Charles E. Cotherman, eds., *Sent to Flourish: A Guide to Planting and Multiplying Churches* (Downers Grove, IL: IVP Academic, 2019).

INTRODUCTION: WHAT DOES A SPIRITUALLY FORMED CHURCH PLANTER LOOK LIKE?

[1]To a point. See Matt Woodley and Bert Crabbe, "A Calling Confirmed," *Leadership Journal*, Fall 2010, www.christianitytoday.com/pastors/2010/fall/callingconfirmed.html.

1. HOW TO BE BOTH A PASTOR AND A PERSON

[1]Zack Eswine, *The Imperfect Pastor* (Wheaton: Crossway, 2015), Introduction.

[2]Chris Adams, lecture delivered at PSWC Celebration, April 20, 2018. See also "Evidence Grows of Problem of Clergy Burnout," *New York Times*, August 2, 2010.

[3]I am indebted to my friend, Pastor Darren Adwalpalker, for his powerful insights on this passage.

[4]For more on essential disciplines, see my chapter, "How to Survive, Then Thrive, in the Midst of the Storm," in *Sent to Flourish: A Guide to Planting and Multiplying Churches*, ed. Len Tang and Charles Cotherman (Downers Grove, IL: InterVarsity Press, 2019).

[5]C. S. Lewis, *A Grief Observed* (New York: Bantam, 1961), 80.

[6]Adams, lecture, April 20, 2018.

2. GROWTH: HOW CAN I PLAN FOR MY OWN SPIRITUAL FORMATION?

[1]Parker Palmer, *Let Your Life Speak: Listening to the Voice of Vocation* (San Francisco: Jossey Bass, 2000), 30.

[2]Dallas Willard, *Renewing the Christian Mind* (New York: HarperOne, 2016), 21.

[3]I'm paraphrasing Dallas Willard, who employs this theme often in his writings. See especially *Spirit of the Disciplines* (New York: HarperCollins, 1988), ch. 9; *The Great Omission* (San Francisco: HarperOne, 2006), ch. 8; *Renewing the Christian Mind* (San Francisco: HarperOne, 2016), ch. 2.

[4]To go deeper into this, I recommend chapter 9 of Ruth Haley Barton, *Sacred Rhythms* (Downers Grove, IL: InterVarsity Press, 2006), and chapter 10 of Peter Scazzero, *Emotionally Healthy Spirituality* (Nashville: Thomas Nelson, 2006).

[5]I give more detail on the practice of these disciplines in *Sent to Flourish: A Guide to Planting and Multiplying Churches*, ed. Len Tang and Charles Cotherman (Downers Grove, IL: InterVarsity Press, 2019), ch. 4.

⁶Phyllis Tickle, *The Divine Hours: Pocket Edition* (New York: Oxford University Press), 2007.

⁷See Gary Thomas, *Sacred Pathways* (Grand Rapids, MI: Zondervan, 2010).

⁸See Willard, *Spirit of the Disciplines*, ch. 10; Barton, *Sacred Rhythms*, 186-87.

⁹Dallas Willard, *Renovation of the Heart* (Colorado Springs: NavPress, 2002), 83.

3. SUFFERING: CAN I EMBRACE A LIFE PEPPERED WITH DIFFICULTY?

¹Quoted in Tish Harrison Warren, *Liturgy of the Ordinary* (Downers Grove, IL: InterVarsity Press, 2016), 122.

²See David T. Olson, *Discovering Your Leadership Style* (Downers Grove, IL: InterVarsity Press, 2014).

³Henri Nouwen, *The Wounded Healer* (New York: Random House, 1979), 4.

⁴Ed Stetzer and Daniel Im, *Planting Missional Churches* (Nashville: B&H Academic, 2016), 162.

4. POWER: DO OTHERS EXPERIENCE ME AS A SAFE PERSON?

¹Richard J. Foster, *The Challenge of the Disciplined Life* (New York: Harper and Row, 1985), ch. 10.

²Quoted in Jamin Goggin and Kyle Strobel, *The Way of the Dragon or the Way of the Lamb* (Nashville: Nelson, 2017), ch. 7.

³Andy Crouch, *Strong and Weak* (Downers Grove, IL: InterVarsity Press, 2016), 170-71.

⁴Crouch, *Strong and Weak*, 170-71.

⁵Brennan Manning, *The Relentless Tenderness of Jesus* (Grand Rapids, MI: Revell, 2004), 44-46.

⁶Eugene Peterson, *Working the Angles: The Shape of Pastoral Integrity* (Grand Rapids, MI: Eerdmans, 1987), 165-66.

⁷Peterson, *Working the Angles*, 165-66.

⁸Peter Scazzero, *The Emotionally Healthy Church* (Grand Rapids, MI: Zondervan, 2010), 7.

⁹Robert E. Logan, *The Church Planting Journey* (Los Angeles: Logan Leadership, 2019), 6.

¹⁰Scot McKnight, *A Community Called Atonement* (Nashville: Abingdon, 2007), 21.

¹¹In Goggin and Strobel, *Way of the Dragon*, ch. 1.

5. OBSCURITY: CAN I MINISTER WITHOUT BEING NOTICED?

¹Brené Brown, *Daring Greatly* (New York: Avery, 2012), 22.

²Association of Religion Data Archives, "Size of Congregation," 2012, www.thearda.com/ConQS/qs_295.asp.

³David A. Roozen, "American Congregations 2015: Thriving and Surviving," Hartford Institute for Religion Research, 2015, http://hirr.hartsem.edu/American-Congregations-2015.pdf. Duke and Hartford break up their size groups differently, but the numbers are compatible.

⁴For more implications of these numbers, see Brandon O'Brien's very helpful *The Strategically Small Church* (Bloomington, MN: Bethany House, 2010), and Karl

Vaters, *The Grasshopper Myth* (newsmallchurch.com, 2013).

[5]Erin Chan Ding, Cathy Norman Peterson, and Tony Gervase, "Centered on Kids," *Covenant Companion*, March 7, 2019, https://covenantcompanion.com/2019/03/07/centered-on-kids/. See also www.lifeformoz.com.

[6]Ed Stetzer, "Are You on Track if You Lead a Church of Less Than 100?," *The Exchange*, February 17, 2017, https://bit.ly/2A8PijF.

[7]Vaters, *Grasshopper Myth*, 6.

[8]Vaters, *Grasshopper Myth*, 51.

[9]Eugene Peterson, *Working the Angles: The Shape of Pastoral Integrity* (Grand Rapids, MI: Eerdmans, 1987), 2.

[10]Dallas Willard, *Spirit of the Disciplines* (New York: HarperOne, 1999), 172-73.

[11]Kevin Haah, in *Starting Missional Churches*, ed. Mark Lau Branson and Nick Warnes (Downers Grove, IL: InterVarsity Press, 2014), 93.

6. FAILURE: AM I RESILIENT IN THE FACE OF SETBACKS AND DEFEATS?

[1]Erwin McManus, *An Unstoppable Force* (Loveland, CO: Group, 2001), 133.

[2]Robert Quinn, *Deep Change: Discovering the Leader Within* (San Francisco: Jossey-Bass, 1996), 3.

[3]Dan Allender, *Leading with a Limp* (Colorado Springs, CO: Waterbrook, 2006), 135.

[4]Eugene Peterson, *The Contemplative Pastor: Returning to the Art of Spiritual Direction*, vol. 17, The Leadership Library (Dallas: Word, 1989), 149-50.

[5]In Mark Batterson, *Primal* (Colorado Springs, CO: Multnomah, 2009), 165.

[6]In Mark Batterson, *Primal* (Colorado Springs, CO: Multnomah, 2009), 165.

[7]Crouch, *Strong and Weak* (Downers Grove, IL: InterVarsity Press, 2016), 174.

[8]AJ Swodoba, in *Starting Missional Churches,* ed. Mark Lau Branson and Nick Warnes (Downers Grove, IL: InterVarsity Press, 2014), 153.

7. PACE: AM I TREATING CHURCH PLANTING LIKE A MARATHON OR LIKE A SPRINT?

[1]For more wisdom from Kurt, I highly recommend Cameron Lee and Kurt Fredrickson, *That Their Work Will Be a Joy* (Eugene, OR: Cascade, 2012).

[2]Alan Fadling, *An Unhurried Life* (Downers Grove, IL: InterVarsity Press, 2013), 9.

[3]Fadling, *An Unhurried Life*, 10.

[4]Terry Walling, "Essentials of Corporate Revitalization," lecture at Fuller Theological Seminary, April 2002.

[5]Fadling, *Unhurried Life*, 16. I also highly recommend Alan Fadling's *An Unhurried Leader* (Downers Grove, IL: InterVarsity Press, 2017).

[6]One of Justin Whitmel Earley's rules is "No Phone Before Bible." See his very helpful *The Common Rule: Habits of Purpose for an Age of Distraction* (Downers Grove, IL: InterVarsity Press, 2019).

[7]Richard Foster, *Celebration of Discipline* (San Francisco: HarperCollins, 1988), 190. See Deuteronomy 14:26 for a tantalizing glimpse of this sort of worship.

[8]I highly recommend Ruth Haley Barton, *Invitation to Retreat* (Downers Grove, IL: InterVarsity Press, 2018).

[9]Abraham Heschel, *The Sabbath* (New York: Farrar, Straus and Giroux, 1979), 75.
[10]Eugene Peterson, *The Pastor: A Memoir* (New York: HarperOne, 2011), 311.
[11]In Fadling, *Unhurried Life*, 122.
[12]Dallas Willard, *The Divine Conspiracy* (San Francisco: HarperCollins, 1998), 62.

8. TEAM: HAVE I RELINQUISHED MY AMBITION TO BE A SUPERHERO?

[1]Bob Logan, *The Church Planter's Toolkit* (Bloomington, MN: ChurchSmart Resources, 1991). I highly recommend Bob's *The Church Planting Journey*, which brings together his forty years of church planting insights.
[2]William Easum, *Sacred Cows Make Gourmet Burgers: Ministry Anytime, Anywhere, by Anyone* (Nashville: Abingdon, 1995), 15.
[3]Easum, *Sacred Cows*, 49.
[4]Steve Sjogren and Rob Lewin, *Community of Kindness* (Ventura, CA: Regal, 2003), 156.
[5]Note the plurality of leaders in Acts 13:1-4 (Antioch); Acts 20:17-38 (Ephesus); 1 Timothy 3:1-13; Titus 1:5-9; Hebrews 13:7, 17; and 1 Peter 5:1-5.
[6]We have been helped greatly here by Ruth Haley Barton, *Pursuing God's Will Together* (Downers Grove, IL: InterVarsity Press, 2012).
[7]John of Damascus, from the English translation of *The Liturgy of the Hours* (4 vols.) © 1974, International Commission on English in the Liturgy Corporation. All rights reserved.

9. CONFLICT: DO I HANDLE DIFFICULT PEOPLE GRACIOUSLY?

[1]I got this question from a talk by business writer Phil Hodges. For more of his wisdom, see Ken Blanchard and Phil Hodges, *The Servant Leader* (Nashville: Thomas Nelson, 2003).
[2]John Stott, *The Message of 2 Timothy* (Downers Grove, IL: InterVarsity Press, 1973), 79.
[3]"Morning Prayer of Philaret of Moscow," available at Holy Trinity Russian Orthodox Church, www.holytrinityorthodox.com/calendar/los/November/19-09.htm.

10. FAMILY: AM I LEADING IN A WAY THAT BRINGS LIFE TO THOSE DEAREST TO ME?

[1]Ajith Fernando, *The Family Life of a Christian Leader* (Wheaton, IL: Crossway, 2016), 95.
[2]Craig S. Keener, *And Marries Another* (Peabody, MA: Hendrickson, 1993), 83.
[3]Kara Powell and Chap Clark, *Sticky Faith* (Grand Rapids, MI: Zondervan, 2011), 23.
[4]Quoted in Justin Whitmel Earley, *The Common Rule: Habits of Purpose for an Age of Distraction* (Downers Grove, IL: InterVarsity Press, 2019), 15.

CONCLUSION

[1]Dallas Willard, *Knowing Christ Today: Why We Can Trust Spiritual Knowledge* (New York: HarperOne, 2009), 211.

ABOUT THE AUTHOR

 **Tim Morey** (DMin, Fuller Theological Seminary; MDiv, Bethel Seminary) is the founding and lead pastor of Life Covenant Church in Torrance, California, and adjunct assistant professor of church planting at Fuller Theological Seminary. He has also served with the Evangelical Covenant Church's national church planting team as an assessor, trainer, and coach, and has taught, coached, and consulted on church planting for other denominations. He is the author of *Embodying Our Faith: Becoming a Living, Sharing, Practicing Church*, and a contributing author to *Starting Missional Churches* and *Sent to Flourish*. He lives in Torrance, California, with his wife and two daughters.

FULLER
CHURCH PLANTING INITIATIVE

EQUIPPING YOU TO PLANT MISSIONAL CHURCHES

Fuller Seminary's Church Planting Initiative prepares men and women to plant and multiply missional churches. Our renowned faculty and experienced practitioners provide you with the healthy root system you'll need to plant a flourishing church that makes disciples and helps transform communities. We believe the three roots needed are (1) a biblical theology of church planting, (2) the spiritual formation of the planter, and (3) the missional skills to reach a post-Christian culture.

Fuller also partners with church planting networks and denominations to equip church planters for kingdom impact. In addition to master's-level church planting courses, Fuller now offers a nonacademic professional certificate in church planting using our interactive digital platform, FULLER Equip.

LEARN MORE AT FULLER.EDU/CHURCHPLANTING OR CHURCHPLANTING@FULLER.EDU.